THE EXIT STRATEGY

PLAN. RECOVER. THRIVE.

GAINA RADFORD

Second edition 2016 | Copyright Gaina Radford

Edited by - Wendy Macdougall, Text Perfection
Photography - Tony Hewitt, Hewitt Photography
Marketing by - Damian Skinner, Ideaium
Book Cover Graphic Design: Fenella Pecotich
Book Layout ©2013 BookDesignTemplates.com

Self-Published
ISBN – 978-0-9944904-1-4
Gaina Radford
www.gainaradford.com

Dedication

I dedicate this book to my magnificent daughter Cait. Without her I would not have had the strength to get through each day during the whole tumultuous ordeal. Every action I took was because I believed and knew that Cait and I both deserved to be happy so that we could be the best version of ourselves.

Table of Contents

ONE

....AND SO IT BEGINS

And so it begins ... universe, give me the words to say to communicate my thoughts, wisdom, humour and possible options to help the separated and divorced of this world.

To give you some more insight about what drove me to write this book, I have to begin by saying that I am a planner. I actually plan for a living - project managing that is. Managing projects, scope, teams, stakeholders and delivery. Putting things in sequential order, allocating resources, assessing risks and issues, adding mitigations around these, adding timelines and ultimately assigning a cost to each task. My occupation helped me get through the most gut-wrenching time of my life - the breakdown of my ten year marriage with my then husband and the years that followed. I planned, counted and allocated a 'percentage complete' to every task. I identified the risks, actions, decisions and issues that I was encountering and put mitigations around them as a coping mechanism.

An example - the last Christmas Day that I would have to spend with his family, counting the hours until I could stop pretending to be happy, say goodbye to them all and have the feeling of relief knowing that I would never have to be placed in that horrendous situation again - ever. Task complete 100%. Tick. Done, done. Then move on to the next task.

I suppose it sounds very clinical, but the methodology that I followed and the mechanics of it all were very therapeutic. Calming and soothing - all of it an act of self-preservation. Looking back now, I'm very proud of what I achieved. It seems like it was a whole other lifetime away. I recall reading somewhere that during times of trauma it is recommended to take one day at a time. How true! Each morning I would wake up ...... hoping that he was already up and out of bed. With my hand on my heart, I would take a few deep breaths and say my daily mantra, "I want more joy in my life".

I am happy to report that after all the pain and anguish of going through this whole process, I now have pure joy in my life. I don't look back and regret the relationship or my decision to get married, as it resulted in my beautiful and brilliant daughter being born, and I gained life-changing wisdom for which I will always be grateful.

So, please take whatever you can from this book. My hope is that it raises your awareness and nourishes your soul in some small way. Enjoy.

Being married to him wasn't a joyous time for me, although it was in the beginning. But as time passed by the relationship did not make me happy - not in the slightest. Of course, I had moments where I had fun and I laughed. But those moments were heavily outweighed by other events and I wasn't the best version of myself with him in my life. I was quite simply soul-destroyed. I wasn't the best mother, daughter, sister, friend or colleague either.

Don't get me wrong - it didn't start off that way. In the beginning it was sensational - the excitement and the quickening of my heartbeat when we met - amazing! The romance, the laughing, the shared interests and the same family background. There were a lot of similarities. After about 18 months of dating, we were married (I was 24 and he was 32). Right after our honeymoon we moved to Canberra because he had taken a new job there. Moving to Canberra was exciting - new husband, new city, new house, new job and friends. I relished the whole idea of starting again and was thrilled at the prospect of new adventures ahead.

I must admit the first time I arrived in Canberra was a bit of a shock. I had this preconceived idea that Canberra would be another Sydney, being that it was Australia's capital city, so you can imagine my shock when I rocked up at the airport that was more regional than domestic, and then after a very short taxi ride, found myself in the northern suburbs surrounded by mountains with farms and sheep! I mean, WTF!! This town is meant to be the capital of Australia and there were sheep and cows in the fucking suburbs! Then whilst in the taxi, to my amusement and astonishment, a fire truck went past me. It wasn't red - it was yellow! You have to ask yourself why? Who the hell thought up that little beauty? I love creativity as much as the next person, but certain things shouldn't be messed with. But I came to appreciate that Canberra was like no other city I had ever known. I learned to love it for its quirkiness.

We settled into life in Canberra and much to my delight Canberra was like a warm embrace. The people were educated, warm, friendly, engaging, passionate, inquisitive, and creative with a quirky sense of sophisticated style.

Three months later I found out I was pregnant, by which time I was 25 years old. The news was welcomed by all the family, in particular my parents and grandma. They were ecstatic and screamed with delight when I told them the news. My brothers were very excited at the prospect of being uncles for the first time.

My pregnancy was overall hassle free, with the exception of a two week period when I experienced morning sickness and couldn't move my sorry arse off the couch for fear of regurgitating the water and crackers that I had just consumed. I seriously thought I was going to die - expire on the couch like a beached whale, with swollen ankles in my PJs. Real nice! I remember thinking how the hell do women around the world do this? It was seriously fucked. For starters, there were bodily changes - the boobs got bigger and went from a DD to an E cup (no complaints there), my skin glowed but my nails, hair and body suffered dramatically (and are yet to fully recover twenty years on).

From the age of 18 till 24 (when I moved to Canberra) I had a French hairdresser named Marc, who loved my hair as it was long, blonde, thick and very straight. Then after I had my daughter I went back to visit him in Perth and the moment he saw me (and my hair) he scoffed - not realising that I had gone through a pregnancy and given birth. He picked up my hair in disgust and said in his heavy French accent, "What have you done to your hair? It is not the same. It is ruined. Where has the thickness gone?"

I told him that I had a baby girl, and he replied, "She has sucked the life out of you".

He was right. Having a baby drains every nutrient out you and all they leave your body with is the discarded crap - charming! But I was more than happy to pay such a dear price for this gift of pure love in my life.

In late October after a few false alarms our little bundle of joy finally arrived. She was named Caitlin and weighed 8 pounds 4 oz, and was 51 cm in length. Truly a beautiful and wondrous baby girl with blonde hair, pale green-blue eyes, perfect ruby red lips, and long, thick, black eyelashes. She brought joy to everybody she came into contact with. All she had to do was smile and everybody fell instantly in love with her. She was (and still is) a very warm, quietly confident and calm presence.

Canberra was where Cait was born and raised for the first five years of her life. We embraced the change of lifestyle, the spectacular seasonal weather and social atmosphere. Canberra was full of well-travelled and educated people with interesting opinions - whether they are about politics, the economy, rugby or current affairs. Canberrans love great food, appreciate a quaffable red wine and thrive on a stimulating debate.

I learnt a lot in Canberra, both personally and professionally. But through the excitement of the new baby, home and job, it soon became apparent that I was living a single parent life, even though I was married. We moved to Canberra for his job (an Economist with the Commonwealth Government) and his job was pivotal to his identity. His job was who he was. It defined him - his place in society. It helped him categorise and slot himself into an imaginary hierarchy that made him comfortable and able to operate.

To me this was very sad. By that I mean what would he do without his job? Be nothing? I don't believe a job defines a person; it is what is inside you that counts, regardless of your occupation. He not only defined himself by his job, on top of that he was a 'smart/stupid'.

Allow me to elaborate and explain - to me there are three kinds of people in this world:

1. Smart/Smart - a person who is street-smart, has commonsense, emotional maturity and is intellectually smart (my recommendation and preference);
2. Smart/Stupid - a person who is intellectually smart, but has no commonsense, is not practical or street smart and is emotionally challenged (not recommended); and
3. Stupid/Stupid - a person who simply has no idea about anything (just don't go there - it's not worth the pain, unless you want a one night stand and they have a rocking body and you don't want them to talk).

So, as he had the characteristics of being a smart/stupid, it caused me no end of grief. On the one hand he could argue and ponder the world's economic workings with his sharp intellect till the cows came home. Yet he struggled to change a light bulb, change a tyre or do any practical DIY jobs around the house. Case in point - if any noise went 'bump' in the middle of the night, it would be me getting up to investigate - not him. There is nothing more unattractive in a man than seeing him still tucked up in bed as you wonder around the house seeing if a burglar is trying to break in. Whatever trace of respect you had for him (and by that stage, it was hanging by a thread) was completely severed. He was completely clueless and in many circumstances I would just look at him in absolute disbelief and think ..... really? I was at a loss as to how he had managed to survive this long without someone smashing his head in. He was just so unaware of his limitations, but had the narcissistic trait of being completely arrogant in his self-belief that he was intellectually superior to the majority of people in the world. This 'feature' of his personality (some might argue that it is a defect) didn't endear him to others either.

He was utterly and completely defined by his work. Work was his life and his comfort zone, and this was reflected in the diminishing amount of time that he spent at home. He worked very long hours, was gruff when he finished work and didn't want to socialise with anyone. This behaviour was all new to me as I am a very social person, with a great network of family and friends. I didn't comprehend why he was acting like this. The previous two years he was happy to go out, to socialise with friends and family and have a great time, and I mistakenly believed this behaviour would continue on post marriage and the birth of our child. But, no, this wasn't to be the case.

Being a resourceful and intelligent woman, my survival instincts kicked in and I reacted by re-balancing and compensating for his behavioural inadequacies. I worked full time, studied at university, and surrounded myself with a great group of friends that became my support system. I was forced to become independent of him and build a life without him because he was never around. I couldn't depend on him being there. If he was there, it was perceived as a bonus. However, in the latter stages of the relationship, it was more of a hindrance.

So, became the routine - get up in the morning and wake Cait from her slumber, prepare and eat our breakfast, drop Cait off to childcare, then drop him off at work. Then I went to work and at the end of the day I would pick Cait and him up, prepare and eat dinner, bath Cait, read her a story and then it would be time to relax and watch a bit of TV or finish university assignments before falling into bed completely exhausted at the end of the day.

The exception was on the odd Friday night when I would go out with friends without him because he didn't want to socialise. And every Sunday Cait and I would go to the Kingston markets and then visit my friends who owned and ran a café in Kingston - the gorgeous Miriana and Janey! It is a rare thing to meet such wonderful people who you know you will be your friends for the rest of your life. Anita, Miriana and Janey supported me throughout the entire ordeal whilst I was in Canberra and still continue to do so years after. They all possess that wonderful sense of mischief and are amazingly strong, intelligent, humourous, inspiring and beautiful women.

I made a conscious effort to make the most of the situation in which I found myself. I took it as an amazing opportunity. I was newly married and had a little girl to consider. I was 25 years old and operating on the traditional model of marriage that my parents used - it was the only example I knew.... at the time.

I was becoming increasingly angry and resentful at the lack of interest, support and engagement from him - it was NOT what I had signed up to. I would ask if he wanted to do more, if he wanted to go out for dinner and do activities - just the two of us - but he wasn't interested. The thought that he might not be interested in me simply did not cross my mind - as I know that might be what you are thinking. But it wasn't that at all. He was still madly in love with me and was very interested in me. But he had detached himself and could only cope with smaller quantities of life at one given time. However, I did not sign up for raising my daughter by myself, not having any emotional support from my husband or any form of comfort or no social life or social activity. This was absolute bullshit and I wanted out. Something had to drastically change. He didn't - or couldn't - so I did.

TWO

....

OUTSOURCING

applied my business logic to my situation and thought what would I do at work? If I needed something that wasn't readily available, I would simply outsource. So, I simply outsourced what I needed. I outsourced emotional support to my family and friends. Humour, companionship, comfort and joy from friends and family. Physical touch through regular massages and having my nails done, combined with hugs from friends and family. I was very creative and outsourced to numerous people - getting what I needed from the various sources to fill the void - outsourcing all that I needed to get me through the day.

But the biggest source of joy was from my daughter, Caitlin. Every time I looked at her she made me happy, knowing that at the very least I had got something beautiful out of the relationship. Cait was my focal point and saviour for the entire duration of the relationship with her father. She continues to ground me and brings me back to my core values if I start to stray from my chosen path.

Yes, I'm waffling on ... and you want me to get to the helpful stuff. Well, I will try and give you some words of advice about different scenarios with possible options and approaches to navigate.

I am going to adopt the SWOT analysis to this (many of you will be familiar with this) - Strengths, Weaknesses, Opportunities and Threats, advantages and disadvantages - but with a sprinkling of interesting stories added to lighten the mood. My writing style is more business-like and direct, so please bear with me. If I have learned anything from the last 11 years of being a single parent, it is that whatever gets you through the day (be that a joke, family, friends, massages, cigarettes, a moment of kindness, a hug, unexpected compliment from a stranger or a grey goose vodka caprioska), then so be it - whatever floats your boat! For me, it was all of the above - and the latter in copious amounts.

Let's begin, shall we? The intent of this book is to share my journey, knowledge and scenarios that I have applied for the duration of the process. They are not necessarily just for the divorced (I don't like that word), but for those who have been in a relationship. I am by no means a psychiatrist, but I am a sexual wellness coach and relationship counsellor and thought I would put my 'pen to paper', because over the years friends have sought my advice on the topic, so I thought it would be worthwhile to document it - hence, this book that you now hold in your hands.

I trust that you take whatever you can from it - be that a smidgeon of advice or some entertaining stories that bring a smile to your face and lighten your heart. I have tried to provide a balanced view from both the male and female perspective. I have spoken with many women and men on the subject and incorporated their views into the chapters, allowing for the majority of the suggestions to be applied to both parties. BTW - I've embraced the use of swear words, so if you take offence to these words, I hope you enjoy replacing them with more palatable ones. Knock yourself out - see it as a word game. If nothing more, it will certainly keep your mind active ☺.

THREE

....

SELF-PRESERVATION

Self-preservation is what kept me sane during the entire experience and I cannot emphasise enough the importance of the act of self-preservation. Out of survival and pure necessity I shut down areas of myself to my then husband with the sole purpose of protecting myself - whether that be the physical, emotional, spiritual and mental or a combination of all of them at the end of the relationship. Coping just one day at a time consumed much of my energy. His negativity and just his breathing alone (yes, I resented his breathing, as I interpreted this as him stealing the oxygen meant for other more worthy candidates) sucked every ounce of energy out of every cell of my being. (I have since moved on from this thought .... just.) I could only cope with one thing at a time, which for a person who is extremely organised and a constant multi-tasker, was a hard thing to get my head around and to accept that I had to operate like this.

So, I applied every ounce of my energy into just getting through each day. It was a struggle to get up, get showered and get ready in the morning. I became mechanical and would switch to autopilot. On reflection, I am not too sure how I managed to survive - it was as if the lights were on, but nobody was at home.

The protective barrier of self-preservation was somehow holding me together, like glue, shielding me from him ....

protecting me from the comments, the nervous energy and anxiety that he was projecting, along with the constant barrage of the underlying criticism. The questioning of why I peeled the potatoes with a sharp knife instead of a peeler; why I vacuumed a certain way; why I squeezed the toothpaste in the middle of the tube; and why I liked the toilet roll to be hanging down from the top and not underneath. My response to all of this questioning was "don't question me".

But why the questions? Who the fuck cares anyway? Is there a right or wrong way to do things? Not generally - just a different way of doing things. It just wasn't his way of doing things, but that didn't mean that they were wrong. They were just different!

Again, this was a control thing that he would try to assert over me, and if that is all he had to complain about, then bloody hell, it's not as if the whole world would come to an end if I squeezed the toothpaste in the middle of the tube! I mean - fuck me - that's just beyond comprehension and not worth wasting any more time thinking about it. That's for him to reconcile with in his own sweet time.

The systematic control theme continued - each comment and action slowly chipping away at me in order for him to feel better about himself. What sort of a person does that to another individual? Some would say a narcissist. But the reality is - not a very happy person!

I am proud to say that I survived each day. When you are in a relationship where you no longer enjoy the other person on any level, you shut down aspects of yourself. Bit by bit I shut down all aspects of myself to my ex, in the belief that he was no longer worthy of my attention. His behaviour made me so miserable that I first shut down my very active and intelligent mind - my ideas, thoughts, wishes, wants, desires, experiences, hopes, dreams and opinions. I think in hindsight, apart from my obvious physical attributes, vivacious and gregarious nature, cheekiness, wicked sense of humour, warmth and great personality, it was my intelligence and quick wit that won him over and what he loved the most about me.

So, this was the first thing that I shut down. It was like I was punishing him. He wasn't getting this from me; he wasn't worthy of me sharing any information with him. He had once remarked at the end of the relationship that I had 'lost my mojo', that I looked vacant when he spoke, that I zoned out and didn't take any notice of him, that I wasn't interested in him physically. I had disputed these facts at the time as I didn't want to give him the satisfaction of being right.

I hadn't lost my mojo at all. I had just lost interest in anything and everything to do with him. So by applying the self-preservation approach, it saved me. Years and years of constant grind wears away at not only your mojo, but also your soul. Fragments of your soul get chipped off and left behind. To put it in simple terms, it is soul-destroying being in a relationship where you are not happy. It slowly but surely wears away your confidence, self-worth, self-esteem, happiness and vibrancy. Everything that you were at the beginning of the relationship - all the attributes you had that attracted your partner and made them fall in love with you - were slowly becoming the things that your partner resented and criticised. Any of this ringing any bells with you?

I have a theory that my ex was attracted to all my qualities - qualities that he, in fact, did not possess. He was a moth to the flame. I was this wild, exquisite creature who was confident, glorious and full of life. Like slow erosion, bit by bit, he started to resent them and made it his mission to destroy these beautiful qualities in me. I'm not sure if this was at a conscious or subconscious level, but nevertheless it was carried out with military precision. He resented that I embodied the qualities that he didn't possess. I was hard-working, confident, engaging, warm, affectionate, inclusive, social, compassionate, sexy, sensual, loyal, caring, successful, earned good coin, well-respected, fearless, joyous and great fun to be around. It was like he was jealous of all these qualities, or was hoping that by being close to me these qualities might rub off on him. It was as if I was the brilliant light and if he stood next to me then he might absorb these qualities.

I am more than aware that people bring different things to the table in a relationship. I am far from perfect, but by bringing the different skills, qualities, strengths to the table a healthy partnership finds a natural balance. This would be a fair assumption, do you think? An example - I am organised and he wasn't. He was brilliant at cooking duck. I wasn't. But the cloud of resentfulness slowly started to thicken around us. Everything should have been 'ticketyboo'. But sadly, no, this wasn't the case.

Throughout the whole marriage and split, my self-preservation shield was applied. The thickness of this shield varied and depended on the activities and my energy levels on the day.

Once we parted, the shield remained, as if I had to be on guard and be prepared for attack at any given moment. That if my defences were down then I'd be open to attack from him, or anybody else who might smell the weakness - like a pack of animals around a wounded animal. I would be targeted and I would be hurt again.

I didn't know how far the next wounding would go. I had a very profound fear that it would be too deep from which to recover. Not only would I be vulnerable, but also I wondered what sort of broken person would I become? I didn't want to end up a blubbering mess on the floor, as I am not that type of woman. I am a strong and magnificent woman and I had to be brave for my daughter. I had an inner knowing and firm belief that what he was saying to me was wrong and simply not true. I refused to believe it. I refused to allow him to take everything from me.

"Yes, it's a well-known fact about you: you're like death, you take everything."

- Milan Kundera, Laughable Loves

It has taken some time for the shield to come down or decrease in thickness. It's been over 11 years now and during that time I have, and continue to, enjoy the company of some absolutely amazing, intelligent and spirited men. But still I think after a great wounding you pause for a moment ...... and are more aware and careful in your decisions. You can't help it. You no longer rush into a relationship head-first with all the excitement that you would have embraced pre-wounding. You still get excited but your cautious ..... just in case - ever watchful. You have moments when you think that this not a fair way of entering a new relationship with the other person, that you are not coming into the relationship on an equal footing, not giving 100% effort. It's not their fault that you are wounded, but the heart is a fragile organ and therefore you have to be the gatekeeper of the amount of love coming and going - for a while at least. For just sometimes you feel that your heart may simply not recover from any more rounds of brutalisation.

The perfect balance is to respect you heart's needs and wants and be aware and communicate this to your new partner. If it's right, then they will be patient and respectful of your needs, as the rewards at the end will be glorious and well worth the investment. Because you are you, after all, in all your magnificence.

....

FOUR

SIGNS THAT THE RELATIONSHIP IS GOING BAD

"They say marriages are made in heaven. But so is thunder and lightning"

– Clint Eastwood

You don't have to be a genius to realise that things are going bad. You feel it, whether it's a gradual thing that slowly builds up or it hits you like a slap in the face. Either way there are degrees of relationships going off the rails, and I found the point in which you decide that things have to change, and you put some action around that decision, will depend solely on the individuals involved. There are many signs that the relationship you are in is going bad. Some of the following may resonate with you:

- Fallen out of love with your partner. I can see the best in most people I meet. Each person has at least one thing that I find attractive, beautiful or unique about them. But when you have been through the process in the following dot points then you simply cannot see any redeeming qualities and you just do not love them anymore. I realise there is a difference between being in love and loving a person. But I was neither.

- One partner gives more than the other. Both people in the relationship need to contribute to the relationship. This contribution needs to continue throughout the relationship, otherwise you will find that there is nothing left except anger, resentment and pain. I am a very giving and generous person and have always given 100% to any relationship. I give my love, time, effort and attention unconditionally. But if the other person in the relationship only takes what you give and gives nothing in return, then it is time to cut your losses.

- Have nothing in common anymore and journeyed on different paths. You don't like the same things or interests. Before you used to have many commonalities and delighted in the things that you had in common. The things that were different in your life seemed interesting to your partner at the time, but sadly not now. It's as if you have subconsciously found activities, food, places to visit, and things to talk about that are now completely different to your partner. In my case I had a thirst for things new and as I grew as a person, I matured and blossomed. He had blossomed before I had met him and yet he remained stagnant. This was charming and acceptable at the beginning of the relationship, but when we failed to grow as a couple, not travelling on the same path, things started to go wrong. As hard as I tried to bring him along with me, he refused. Perhaps he was incapable of growing, was fearful or just not interested in making the effort.

- Feel you need to change who you are to make your partner happy (this will lead to disaster). I have witnessed this from a lot of friends who are in relationships. I have a friend in Sydney who as an individual is an amazingly strong, intelligent and beautiful woman. She has a great life and job, and her life is full of interesting things. As a single woman she is true to herself and what I call "single Louisa". But when she meets a man she immediately loses her identity and is completely absorbed by the man and instantly morphs into the person that he wants to her to be. She soon quickly adopts his views and interests and thoughts. If and when she is allowed out to catch up with friends, he is the whole topic of conversation. Don't get me wrong, she presents as being happy as she is in love and in a state of blissful infatuation.

But this type of relationship is all consuming and isolating, which is very dangerous because when/if it fails, she is then left to pick up the broken pieces of her life with few people around her who still love her, as she has alienated everybody whilst in the relationship with him. She is completely and utterly gutted when the relationship fails. She is lost and devastated. She cannot comprehend how she came to this end. She then spends the next few months dissecting and reliving the relationship to ascertain and pinpoint what went wrong - trying to reconcile if she could have done anything differently, or noticed anything sooner, to change the predicted ending of the relationship. And then she embarks on the grieving process, the outcome of which she states that she will never do that again with the next man. But she does. This pattern of behaviour goes far deeper, which one day she will gain enough strength to face, address and conquer. But "single Louisa" is more spectacular than in a "relationship Louisa". Hopefully, one day she will be in a relationship and still remain the beautiful "single Louisa".

- Pick a fight about anything, just because you can. It passes the time and lets you vent your frustrations. I suppose it's a way of sabotaging the relationship sub-consciously - you know that you shouldn't, but you just can't stop yourself. The poisonous words just flow out of your mouth like daggers, or in some circumstances - machetes. You instinctively know what words wound your partner the most, yet the filter from your brain to your mouth has gone on holiday and the words come out with devastating results. To add insult to injury you are unable to resolve the conflict that you and your partner just experienced. In the past you had the negotiation skills of an expert lawyer with a bag of tricks that you could pull out in these situations, such as bargaining, compromise, a joke to defuse the situation or through some hot passionate sex into the mix. But not this time - you just don't care enough to go through all this to resolve the situation.

- Fake it in ALL areas of the relationship and I mean ALL aspects. You fake being happy, you fake the love, you fake the sex, and you smile still when your friends ask you how you are going. Because if you don't smile and say "I'm good", then this would then open you up to a barrage of questions and you haven't processed your current situation enough, let alone speak to your nearest and dearest about it - fearful that if you did you would just simply break down and your pack of cards would fall.

- Any form of touch from them makes you feel physically sick to your stomach. I realise that this may seem a bit extreme to some people, but it's true. You can't help it. It's out of your control, and you simply can't, or won't, fake it anymore. It's hard to comprehend that this was the same person who you ached to have touch you when the relationship was good. The mere touch of this same person excited you beyond belief and stirred up emotions such as love, sexuality, passion and sensuality. It is a cruel twist of fate. For me, this is the only instance where time does not heal old wounds.

So much was my revulsion of his touch that I would go to drastic measures to avoid him. I would either go to bed earlier than him or later than him and pretend to be asleep to avoid any physical contact. I'm a very physical person, so with every inch of my being I just couldn't have him touch me - my body would simply recoil from his. I longed for the day when I wouldn't have to be in his presence. I just couldn't think of anything worse than my ex hugging, kissing or touching me. I think if you have managed to split in an amicable manner, then this scenario may differ. And given time, you are perhaps happy to give them a hug and kiss on the cheek, to say hello and goodbye. But for me it is simply a big fat 'no'.

- Avoid making any plans together. It's fair to say that you go out of your way to make as many plans as possible with everybody else, except your partner. You don't want to spend any time together. You are like ships in the night just passing each other, avoiding any form of contact. I avoided making holiday plans, buying tickets to concerts or events in the future, because I didn't want the hassle of being alone with him - going to the event, sitting during the event and coming home with him in the car. So, no plans were made. (It was bad enough that the mandatory events occurred during this timeframe, like birthdays and Christmas.) I actually went to the other extreme and made alternative plans so that I could get away and not have to spend any time with him. So, I would go to the movies with friends, work longer hours, and had family gatherings with my family that I knew he didn't want to attend. But I also didn't want to be tied down with plans with him just in case I snapped in the heat of the moment - and said, 'no more'.

- When you go out for dinner, you look at anything or anyone other than your partner. I recall a time when Miriana and Cait and I went for dinner down in Margaret River years ago at a restaurant. I spotted a married couple across from us and they didn't talk, or look at each other or engage in any activity. The dinner was clinical and cold. There was no love shown, no look of endearment or anything. It was very sad. I looked at them and I thought how horrible it would be to be in that position - to be in a relationship where you just exist and tread water. I didn't want to be in that position - ever. They had nothing at all to say to each other. Even the waitress felt very uncomfortable serving them. The uncomfortable silence that enveloped them filtered out to the other people in the restaurant. The only conclusion I could make from this is that they were too afraid to split; that they chose to continue in a horrible existence instead of being alone.

- Stop communicating with each other and stop listening to the noise that comes out of their mouth, which is often referred to as 'select deafness'. My late grandfather applied this methodology to perfection. I have to say that my grandparents were very happily married and they loved each other very much. It was just that my granddad just needed some 'alone time'. He was considerably deaf in both ears, thanks to be being torpedoed numerous times during his active duty in WWII. Consequently, his hearing wasn't the best and he sported a hearing aid. He would, on occasion, simply turn the hearing aid off so that he couldn't hear my grandmother talking. This drove my grandmother insane in the beginning, but she soon accepted it and used it to her advantage. It worked for both parties and they lived a very long and happy life together. But to stop communicating is a by-product of your level of unhappiness as you are unwilling to share your thoughts, dreams, feelings ..... anything really, as I didn't think he was worthy of receiving any information from me. For me, I resorted to muttering underneath my breath when he spoke to me. This is childish behaviour, I know, but effective as I expressed my views and released the anger building up inside me like a slow valve being released.

- You don't care what happens to your partner. Your empathy and compassion go out the window when it comes to your partner. Your care factor is a big fat zero. A classic example is when you have a 'weekend warrior' partner (I apologise in advance for my observations on this subject, but they only pertain to my ex-husband and not the general 'weekend warrior' population. I acknowledge that the majority of weekend warriors are ensuring that they have a physical release which is very important - they are having a go, socialising and trying to keep fit and have passion for something, which is very honourable. And I also appreciate the dedication of a body striving to be fitter and firmer ☺).

The term 'weekend warrior' refers to my ex who thought that he was still in the prime of his sporting life and had the sporting ability of a 19 year old with the stamina and sporting prowess to match. Note: this was his ego talking. Sadly though, the mind had failed to inform the body that it was, in fact, completely fucked! That all those years of sporting injuries, carrying my daughter around, working long hours sitting in front of a computer, too much good food and wine and general wear and tear over the years, had finally caught up with his body. So, when he ventured onto the sporting arena he did little or no warm up of the muscles as his ego was still thinking that he still had it going on. To make matters worse, the weekend warriors' sporting teams are now made up of a mix of people aged in their mid 20s, 30s, 40s and some 50s. And to add insult to injury he was now regarded as a 'veteran or master' or graded as B, C or D capability. Not the A grade as he was in his glory days. But your weekend warrior is up against the very fit and firm 19 and early 20 year olds that are at the peak of their physical sporting ability. This equates to:

Weekend Warrior v 19 year old Hottie = WARRIOR INJURY

So, when your weekend warrior dislocates his shoulder, ankle or knee you might find yourself not demonstrating any form of compassion and uttering words like "Oh, for fuck's sake it doesn't hurt that much - have some panadol, put a cold pack on it and stop whining" or "suck it up, princess". This attitude surprises you as you are normally a very caring and compassionate person, but that was then and this is now.

- You prefer roast pumpkin instead of having sex with your partner. Don't laugh. I worked with a woman years ago when I was in my early 20s who had been married for over 30 years. She once commented that she preferred to eat roast pumpkin instead of having sex with her husband. I did think at the time why doesn't she simply combine the two? Bake the pumpkin and have him eat it if off her breasts whilst having sex. But no, she was adamant that pumpkin was her favourite, as it didn't require any mess and she didn't have to shave her legs or bikini line. Surprisingly, she remained happily married. But I did wonder if her husband hated pumpkin!

- Your partner is controlling your life. This includes, but is not limited to, your finances, social interaction with others, decisions on what you wear and what (and how much) food and drink you consume.

- Social interaction - The control of what friends and family you are 'allowed' to see has far reaching implications as this behaviour isolates you from those who love you. The outcome is that you have no other place to turn to and become increasing dependent on your controlling partner, which is just how they like it. So, to them it's a win/win, but it spells complete disaster for you. This is simply unacceptable. Get out of the relationship - this behaviour is not healthy. It saddens me to admit that I have too many friends in this situation. There is one in particular whose husband doesn't like her associating with friends or family who may have different opinions to his. If I call, he asks, "who is on the phone?" and then tells his partner to get off the phone. I'm pleased that she says 'no' and stands up to him, but nevertheless the constant pushback wears on her. Her partner fears that one of her friends or family will convince her to divorce him. Another friend's partner actively bags her friends and family and twists what they say so that it creates a seed of doubt in her mind. I could go on and on with examples, but all the control issues are based on a platform of fear and insecurities from the other partner. Or they are just in a relationship with a narcissist or bully. And if your partner is willing to acknowledge this and work towards addressing this issue, then that's great. There is a hope. But if this is all driven by ego, then you need to decide to move on asap.

- Finances - Well, where to start with this one? A lot to cover here. Does your partner watch every cent that you spend? Do they question your spending habits? Do you hide your receipts of purchases? Hide your purchases in the wardrobe?

Take the tags off your purchases and just hang them in the wardrobe like they have been there all the time? When asked by your partner if a particular item is new, do you respond by saying "No, I've had this in the wardrobe for ages". Sound familiar? Do you have a joint account? Does your partner give you an allowance? It is important to note the difference between watching your budget and spending limits, which is understandable. But watching the finances as a control mechanism based on fear is not good.

- Diet and Exercise - Again, this is a form of control and fear behaviour by your ex. I know too many people whose partners comment on the amount of food and drink they consume, with comments like "Are you sure you need to eat/drink that?" This creates a whole level of self-doubt in the person. A friend of mine is 170cm tall, slim, and athletic and just a beautiful woman. She goes to the gym every day and eats very healthily. Yet her partner is always onto her about her weight and says that she looks fat in particular outfits. I am at a loss to explain this, as he himself is not a fine figure of a man. He has a beer gut, doesn't exercise and eats rubbish, yet he thinks that he has the right to question her body shape/image. I just hope one day she gets the strength to fight back. But as she says, "she chooses her battles ..... she might lose this battle .... but will win the war". This issue is not one she is willing to address .... just yet.

- Bad-mouthing your partner in front of other people and putting them down to make you feel better. This is simply not good on any level as the recipient feels shattered and humiliated and the people around you feel embarrassed, resulting in the person who is doing the bad-mouthing looking like a complete dick.

- Resentment sets in on all levels with your partner. You start saying, "Why can't you just be like such and such a person?" You compare your partner with others and find faults in all that they do. The resentment builds up to a level of disgust in the person and can very easily lead to hatred. Everything that your partner does makes you dislike them more. You no longer see any good or positives in your partner.

- You don't trust your partner in any way. This could be as simple as not trusting in them making decisions, to the other extreme of them cheating on you, or interpreting them looking at other people as if they have slept with them.

- You start to lie about what you are doing, where you are going and who you are seeing, which builds a level of mistrust in the relationship. From speaking to many people follow this behaviour pattern, they aren't actually doing anything that is untoward or untruthful. A friend just goes for a run to get away from his partner for a few hours so that he can think and have some free time, as he feels smothered by her constant calls and lack of trust.

- You stop asking if they love you or saying you love them. This was something that my ex acknowledged after we had split. We used to play a game where I would ask him if he loved me. But halfway through the relationship I stopped asking him. I knew that he did still love me, but I didn't feel anything for him, so I didn't want to play the game anymore and be put in that situation where I would have to respond to this level of questioning. My ex wrote a letter to me after we had split. It was very long letter (about 20 pages) that expressed all his feelings and failings. Again, it was too little too late. One of the things that he mentioned is that he had only just twigged that I had stopped talking about what I was doing in my day and he should have seen this as a sign that the relationship was turning bad. But this was too late - his timing was way off.

- Emotional infidelity - This topic has various layers and is open to interpretation. Through my research I have found that the majority of people concluded that even the thought of wanting to sleep with another person was enough to be classified as infidelity, regardless of whether this notion was followed by physical activity. They saw this as enough of a betrayal. Interestingly enough, many commented that noticing other people should not be classified as emotional infidelity. I agree. One friend claimed, "I'm not dead! Of course I'm going to notice an attractive person who walks past. It doesn't mean I am going to act on it. I'm happily married." He equated it to appreciating some beautiful piece of art in a gallery. But there is a difference between appreciating and drooling over another person and actively commenting on how cute that person is in front of your partner. That is just not cool.

A number of people actively found solace with other people, not physically, but chatting with work colleagues or found friends with whom they could talk to about what was going on in their lives. They found this comforting; that they were able to discuss topics with others and find other people who were different from their partner to fill a gap that their partner wasn't fulfilling - be that talking about sport, architecture (yes, architecture!), their family, work issues or financial problems. Could this be another form of outsourcing? On many occasions they said that they didn't want to worry their partner about issues and so that is why they sought friendships elsewhere. I think it is naïve to assume that one person can provide 100% of what you need (but I have yet to be corrected), even if you are just seeking a difference of opinion (like you would going to see a doctor about a medical issue). But I think the difference for me is when you become emotionally involved and start to think, "what if?" and that there could be more to this person than you initially thought and want to progress and see what direction it could go.

- Addictive behaviour - This would relate to an excess of anything. Such things as alcohol and porn can be enjoyed in moderation, but when abused and consumed in excessive amounts, then this is a cause for concern. I would seek professional help with this point, in particular, as demonstrating an addictive behaviour towards anything requires further investigation. I am only scratching the surface with my opinion here and I don't profess to be an expert on this subject, but from past experience I have found that people can find solace in alcohol, drugs, excessive amount of porn etc, as they are not happy in a particular area of their lives and are trying to suppress thoughts and/or emotions.

- Physical violence – In my personal opinion any form of physical violence shown towards another person is a deal-breaker. The fact that anybody can resort to this is simply unacceptable. A partner's use of violence will no doubt relate to many circumstances from their past, with the only method of expressing frustration being that of a physical release. I realise there are anger management courses that are very good and have a high level of success, but I wouldn't be able to forget (forgive - yes), that this event occurred. Should an argument break out in the future, that thought and fear would always be at the back on my mind and I would be thinking, "he might hit me again". That is something that I couldn't live with. There are varying levels of anger in everybody - from shouting, to letting off steam and hitting out and punching a hole in the wall or kicking a door in. Again, physical violence towards another person that makes that person feel uncomfortable is unacceptable.

Feeling anger is not the same as experiencing physical violence. A friend once told me that that 'anger was a wasted emotion'. I disagree with this statement. Anger is a very real emotion that everybody feels at some point in his or her life. I get angry at big things like social injustice, bigotry, racism, rudeness and anybody who harms children or animals. And I get angry at the little things, too, like someone who puts burnt and used matches back into the matchbox with the unused ones. What matters is how anger is expressed, processed and worked through. It must be done so in a safe and non-confronting way.

- One of the biggest tell-tale signs for me was that I was growing as a person and he wasn't and that he was becoming increasingly stagnant, not learning, experiencing or willing to try new things. He was essentially not participating in life - just observing. This was a sign that our relationship was falling apart, which for a person who is extremely inquisitive with a lively intellect, was not only frustrating, it also deeply saddened me. It was like I was leaving him behind, instead of him walking side by side with me on our journey. It was as if he was struggling to stay afloat with what life was throwing at him - work, home life and everyday existence. Anything else or any additional demands would push him over the edge, as if life was overwhelming in its current state.

I think on reflection that different people have very defined coping capabilities. I can manage and process multiple things at once. I'm always on the move. You can throw a lot of things at me and I'm able to manage. Of course, there are times when I am exhausted and I burn the candle at both ends. I then retreat and look after myself more with the 'care and repair' routine. But generally I am resilient and balanced. I very rarely get overwhelmed by anything. So, you can perhaps understand that when he wouldn't engage in my interests or try new things, the gap started to widen. I would then try new things by myself or with Cait or friends. I developed new interests and did new activities; I wanted to experience everything that life had to throw at me. I loved meeting new people; having chats to them about their experiences and life stories. I embraced people who had a different perspective on life and was intrigued by it all. But every time that I tried to bring my husband in on the journey, he refused. He wasn't interested. So, bit by bit I stopped asking if he wanted to join me, as I just knew the answer would be a 'no'. Having different interests and having your own life is a good thing and a healthy thing for a relationship. That way you have something to talk about at the end of the day. But not being interested or asking questions in what your partner does or doesn't do is a completely different matter. It's like they don't matter. Is it a fear thing that they are clinging to only what they know, and have a fear of moving forward?

- Avoidance is a much-understated action. This is what I applied for quite a few years at the end of the relationship. I kept busy for most of the time. I worked longer hours, did activities after work, like working out at the gym, walking the dog, yoga, and taking my daughter to events. Basically, I did anything to avoid him, to not engage with him - working late at night and on the weekend or movies and dinners with my family, friends and work colleagues. I waited for him to go to sleep before I retired to the bedroom. The whole sleeping in the same bed scenario caused me no end of grief. It wasn't until I left him that I realised the experience of 'a good night's sleep'. For years I slept as far away as possible, perched on the edge of the bed, with every muscle in my body tense and on high alert. For me, because my heart, mind and soul had shut down to him, his physical presence absolutely repulsed me. I couldn't bear for him to touch me; everything about him annoyed and disgusted me. So, when it was time to go to bed, one of two things would happen. The first thing was that I would go to bed early and try to fall to sleep before him. If I didn't, then I would pretend to be asleep when he got into the bed.
- Your children are miserable. I think above all else what validated my decision to ask my husband to leave was my daughter asking each and every each morning, "Is daddy in a good mood today?" This statement alone broke my heart. The fact that she was acutely aware that her dad behaved in such a manner, and her first thought of the day was wondering what mood her daddy was in, was shattering to me as a mother. I

had to get out of the relationship that was impacting my daughter's happiness.

- Seeing your partner shaving his legs in the bath. I know that this may seem a bit extreme, but everybody has his or her breaking point. Some things simply should not be displayed in front of others. My personal breaking point came when I saw my ex-husband shave his rather lithe and lathered legs in the bath - not sexy! When questioned, he responded by saying, "I'm a cyclist. I need to shave them". This very unattractive image has been burnt into my memory forever.
- That you just want out. It's as simple as that. You're done.

....

FIVE

GRIEVING A FAILED RELATIONSHIP

Grieving a relationship is a very powerful and important process. I've related this to the five stages of grieving the death of a loved one. I've experienced loved ones who have passed on, and on researching the topic, I related to the various stages of grieving and I found for me that these could be applied to the death of a relationship. It is very much like a death. The only difference is that the person in question is obviously still alive and walking around. I found that grieving is a very personal process that differs from one person to the next. Some people grieve at the end of the relationship and go into complete shock as they didn't see it coming. The rather obvious signs were there, but they just avoided acknowledging them as it was too real, too raw; or they were hoping that the problems would simply go away. Some just stick their head in the sand, don't want to deal with the emotions and compartmentalise them by putting them in a little box (within another box and another). Like too many people I know, the box of emotions never gets dealt with and are suppressed for a lifetime. With every other emotion, the experience gets compounded and results in a steady build up over the years. But my experience has found that these emotions have a habit of erupting (like a volcano) when the individual least expects or wants it, which can have devastating results for all involved. So I have grouped the stages of grieving into five.

Stage One - Denial and Isolation

In the early stages of marriage after my daughter's birth the denial and isolation of stage one kicked in. The overwhelming emotions that I was starting to feel made me numb. This is not what I had signed up to. I was in this marriage alone. It was all one-sided. I was quietly devastated as this idea of marriage in which I was participating was not what I had perceived it to be. I had based the relationship on the genetic blueprint of those marriages around me when I was a child, which, in hindsight, was naive of me. But at 24 years of age I did the best I could with what knowledge, experience and skills I had at the time. My operating model was standard and not as sophisticated and upgraded as it is now. I felt alone. I went through the motions of everyday life trying to reconcile how I was feeling with how I thought a marriage should be from observing those relationships around me of friends and family. These relationships were based on trust, compassion, and fun, support of each other, love, and generosity of spirit, encouragement, laughter and mutual appreciation of each other. What life I was living contained little or none of those qualities in my marriage. The fact that I had moved to Canberra from Perth added to the feeling of isolation, albeit of a geographical nature. I had some amazing friends around me in Canberra like Miriana and Janey and my family and friends interstate and overseas who were only a phone call away. My best friend, Anita, was still in Perth and was as supportive and encouraging as always.

Stage Two - Anger

The anger was slowly building up in me and due to my frustrations at the time, emerged as demonstrations of defiance and small acts of revenge (I'll get to those later). I couldn't help myself. The anger had to be released; I had to slowly let off steam bit by bit, fearful that if I didn't, I would just explode. I had a deep-seated fear that I was unsure just how far I would go and might reach the point of no return, which wouldn't be beneficial to anybody. I felt like I was an animal that was cornered and had to come out fighting. I became deeply resentful of him and his total disregard of the situation. He was acting fine. He was blissful in his own operating rhythm, happy to exist in this manner, which was a cause for concern in itself. And it was just that - existing and not living. Going to work, which he loved, coming home and spending time with his wife and daughter and then doing the run of the mill activities on the weekend. Come Monday, and you hit the replay button - like groundhog day. Same, same - every fucking week. I mean, really?? How could anybody be happy with this scenario? But it seemingly worked for him. Maybe this was based on the genetic blueprint from his family. Who knew at the time and ultimately who the fuck cared? To outsiders we were the picture-perfect family with two successful professional parents and a beautiful daughter. But as the saying goes, you don't know what happens behind closed doors. I was becoming more and more resentful of him and the pain that he was causing. Then I would feel guilty for being angry, as nobody had forced me to marry him, which made me even angrier as I only had myself to blame for this decision. It was a vicious circle like playing a song on a continuous loop.

But there were warning signs that the universe was giving me. A couple of weeks before the wedding I was driving home from work and I had a car accident. Another vehicle ran through a red light and sideswiped me. This resulted in a black eye from the sun visor and a 30 cm x 5 cm bruise across my chest from the seat belt impact. I got married with a truck load of concealer being applied to my eye and chest. I should have interpreted this as a sign that I wasn't meant to get married. To add to this wonderful gift of hindsight, my Dad did something that I will never forget. In the car on the way to the church on my wedding day, he sat next to me in the back seat of a silver Rolls Royce Phantom. It was a warm, November day and he grabbed my hand and squeezed it very tightly the whole journey.

Then he turned to me and said, "You know, you don't have to get married if you don't want to. You can cancel if you want. I won't be mad if you change your mind. I mean are you really sure that you want to go ahead with marrying him? Don't worry about the cost of the wedding".

I was very shocked at this statement from my Dad, as he is a man of few words and I know that he loves me unconditionally (as does my Mum). But I replied, "Yes, Dad. I want to get married", and he just nodded and cried all the way to the church.

However, I stand by my decision. I don't regret getting married as I received two things. One being the very magical and irreplaceable gift of my beautiful daughter who I love so much. Secondly, being married made me realise that I am an unbelievably strong woman and I can survive absolutely anything the world can throw at me.

Without the marriage and the divorce I would never have gone on my journey of self-discovery, have written my book or found more joy in life.

Stage Three - Bargaining

The next phase of the grieving process is bargaining. I didn't think that this applied to me in the purest form ... like bargaining with the universe (or whatever God you acknowledge) for your partner to be saved and allowed to live. More like bargaining for the relationship to be saved. Secretly, we may make a deal with God or our higher power in an attempt to postpone the inevitable. This is a weaker line of defence to protect us from the painful reality that the relationship is, in fact, over.

But I would see more options being traded in my mind. I was feeling vulnerable and needed to regain some sort of control in my life. What had I done wrong in the relationship? What could I have done differently? Could I be a better person towards him? I started to reflect internally to see what could be changed. I thought I'm no quitter, so I would give it a good shot and have another talk with him to see what can be achieved.

I sat him down on numerous occasions and ran through how unhappy I was feeling and identified what was going wrong. I poured my heart out to him in the hope that he could understand my pain and show some compassion towards the situation. I even suggested that we go and see a marriage counsellor to see if they could help. His response was simply, "There's nothing wrong with me. It must be you, so if you want to go to see a counsellor, then go".

My heart sank. This response demonstrated that he clearly didn't care about our relationship or our family unit. Since the divorce, I now know that he did, in fact, care and loved me very deeply, but he was petrified that by discussing the issues with a counsellor might perhaps reveal deeper issues, like opening Pandora's Box - issues that he had managed to avoid addressing for the last 40 years of his life. Issues which related to our relationship, but had emotionally crippled him enough for him to sacrifice his family life in favour of hiding from them. If only he had the courage to face, address and conquer his demons from his past, which was negatively impacting on his current life and inevitably his future state.

I will admit that on one occasion he made some progress (albeit for a period of two months) but regrettably he went back to his old way of operating, which was his comfort zone. It was heart-breaking. But I had my answer: he wasn't capable of changing, not for me, not for his daughter and not for himself.

Stage Four - Depression

This topic in itself is a very complex one. I am by no means a psychologist, but the rollercoaster of emotions that I experienced during and after the relationship was profound and life changing and cannot be understated. I am a glass half full sort of woman (or overflowing in many cases) - upbeat, happy, positive, loving, fiery, intelligent, compassionate, loyal, fun, joyful, and loves to laugh. So the stresses over the term of the relationship caused me extreme waves of deep sadness. I wouldn't go as far as to say that I went into a deep depression, but the notion of losing the traditional family unit, which was an ideal that I had been raised to believe to be my chosen path in life, was what impacted me the most. I was mourning the loss of the marriage - not him. My world stopped spinning. I felt numb. It was as simple as that.

It wasn't just the feeling that the relationship between husband and wife had died. It was much broader than that. What was I to do now? It was as if a dark cloud had engulfed me and I couldn't see any way of feeling the sunshine on my face ever again. But then I would say to myself, "I want more joy in my life". Then look at him and know I wasn't going to get it from him - ever.

So it took a while to realise that I was responsible for my own happiness and that I should not be dependent on another human being to be the source of that happiness. This was a very tough and valuable life lesson.

I have seen a lot of people dive into a deep depression following the loss of a relationship. Some are unable to recover or move on for months or years on end. I suppose with deep love comes deep loss. I don't think it's fair that people comment on how long it takes for a person to recover. You cannot put a timeframe around it. I have known friends who have taken many years to recover from a partner. They barely function during this time and are not ready to engage or even look at another person in a mentally healthy way. The relationship is simply over, but they can't let go.

My advice is to help and support your friend during this time - a comforting hug can go a long way. You may never understand what emotions your friend is going through as this is a deeply personal experience, but you can be there for comfort and support. You need to feel the grief so that you can heal. You have to go through the darkness to appreciate the light. As the great American poet Mary Oliver wrote:

"Someone I loved once gave me a box full of darkness. It took me years to understand that this too, was a gift"

I have a friend who is an absolute knockout. She is stunningly beautiful. When she goes out with her friends to bars and social events, not one guy will come near her as she has this 'leave me alone' vibe about her, or as I call it, it's like she has a tattoo on her forehead that says 'fuck off'. She was in no way shape or form willing or able to connect with another person. It took all her courage to frock up and get ready to go out that night with her friends. As times passed the 'fuck off' tattoo faded and she got the sparkle back in her eyes - and then it was 'watch out world!'

Stage Five - Acceptance

Reaching this stage of mourning was monumental for me. I had tried everything to make the relationship work. I had gone through the grieving phases and the thought came into my head that I deserved to be happy and that he didn't make me happy. I wasn't going to deny myself joy any longer. He just wasn't the one for me. He just didn't get me. As Elbert Hubbard said:

"He who does not understand your silence will probably not understand your words."

I just accepted that the relationship was over and it was time to move on. This decision takes courage and determination. But once I made the decision I felt elated, and with it came a feeling of immense calm. I knew I was going to be OK. I withdrew from everyone to harness my energy and strength for the last hoorah. As in the final stages of death, I wanted the final stage to be handled with dignity and grace.

So, I was confident in the knowledge that I had done everything that I could before I walked away. I knew I would never look back and wonder. Or worse still, have my daughter say I never tried hard enough to keep the family unit together. I think reaching this point gives you confidence, knowing that you have considered every possible angle to salvage the relationship, but to no avail. The only option left to you is to tell your partner it's over.

You may well have gone through the steps of grieving, but your partner may have been oblivious to your whole process and journey.

SIX

....

RELATIONSHIP ENTRY AND EXIT CRITERIA

Every relationship that you experience has entry and exit criteria. To enter a relationship you have a list of minimum criteria that your potential partner needs to meet. The list differs depending on your circumstances and stage of life that you are in. You decide what are your needs and desires - like the essential criteria such as being a wonderful person who loves sex. And then adding as many 'nice to haves' as possible, such as an appreciation of rugby union, the ocean, cars, great food and a perfectly mixed caprioska, an adventurous spirit and love for art house cult classic films such as the French *Delicatessen* (1991) and Australian *Harvie Krumpet* (2003), *Bad Boy Bubby* (1993) and *Cosi* (1996).

It's interesting that what I wanted and needed at 24 years of age differs greatly from what I need and want today. Like a fine wine, your taste matures after experiencing a few relationships.

I think to execute the exit criteria for a relationship you must first appreciate the entry criteria that you had when you went into the relationship. Has your criteria changed? Do items hold the same value as they used to?

Entry Criteria

The entry criteria for a man to be in my life would be (but not limited to) below:

- Love me as I am and doesn't want to change me.
- Loves my daughter and at least likes my family and friends.
- Is a smart/smart.
- Enjoys a very healthy and varied sex life.
- Sensual and sexual.
- Romantic.
- Shares the same values as me.
- Emotionally mature.
- Masculine.
- Physically impressive - he has to be tall - over 6ft tall with a rugby-type body.
- Intelligent.
- Has a mischievous twinkle in the eyes.
- Great sense of humour that can make me laugh - as not many people can.
- Can cook and clean (when needed).
- Honest, kind, acts with integrity and is compassionate.
- Loves animals.
- Passionate.
- Has faced and conquered his demons - so not a project to fix.
- Is a self-starter with drive and determination.
- A gentleman (when warranted).
- Is fun to be around.
- Can handle himself in most situations with grace and dignity.
- Loves entertaining.
- Is an evolved soul.
- Open minded.
- Dependable.
- Good with his hands (can fix stuff around the house).
- Is single and available.
- Has a healthy mind.
- No ego.

- Isn't a drug addict, alcoholic, angry or violent.
- Will support me in all my endeavours.
- Loyal.
- Sensitive.
- Generous with his time.
- Good communicator.
- Will offer to make me a cup of tea in the middle of the night, if I wanted one.
- Makes me both purr and roar.

We have the tendency to over complicate life with our wants and desires. Or is it just that we just won't settle for anything less than the mandatory items on our lists?

I just want a good man. I am on the camp that some would say I have high standards. But be that as it may, but I'm not willing to put up with anything less. I would rather be by myself. My life is full as it is. I'm not looking for a partner to complete me, as I am a complete person in myself. But it has taken me a very long time to get to this point in my life. I'm after a partner to complement me and enrich my life. A companion to share my life - an equal that makes me roar!

Exit Criteria

To exit a relationship requires a lot of thought, and there must be definite warning signs that things are going bad. So refer to the previous chapter. Well, this came down to the fact that I was done. It was simple as that. So I would often wipe my hands (like I was bushing dirt from my hands) and say to myself, that I was done. It was a very physical reminder that I couldn't and wouldn't continue. I was comfortable in the knowledge that I had tried every possible option, but to no avail. I had offered to go to marriage guidance sessions; had stepped through and evaluated all the pros and cons and the ramifications of my actions. Basically, I conducted a full SWOT analysis of my relationship and I carefully considered what the outcome would mean for my daughter and me.

Emotionally - The panic would set in and I would think 'it is just me being solely responsible for my daughter's full development. I would have to play both the mother and father roles!!......what the fuck have I done?'. The full weight of the situation hit me like a ton of bricks. It was a massive responsibility and I would have to pull out all the stops to do this.

Millions of questions started running through my head. What if I fucked it up? What if my daughter turned out a complete emotional mess? What if she ended up hating me? Or blamed me for the breakup of the family unit? Became one of those kids who is out of control and hates the world?

What if, what if, what if?? This thought process was not doing me any favours. Immediately I made a conscious decision that this destructive thought process would have to stop. I did not have the luxury to entertain the 'what ifs' anymore. If I allowed my thought patterns to go down this 'what if' road, I wouldn't achieve anything in life. I instantly knew that I had the skills to pull this off; that I could raise my daughter flying solo. I mean I had managed to mould a perfectly balanced nine year old little girl so far. So, what if it was just me? I clicked into work mode and looked at my qualities that I would bring to the full parent job description - I was smart, flexible, sensible, compassionate, caring, fearless, protective, mentally tough, emotionally stable, could cook and clean and run a household. I was fun, thought outside of the box, I multi-skilled, was great at entertaining, loved sport (well watching rugby union – does that count?), was social with demonstrated capability. I was emotionally balanced and fit and healthy.

Most of all I loved her more than anything in the world, so if all else failed, then there would be massive amounts of love between us. I met all the criteria to look after my daughter and as I was a quick study. I could learn new things on the job and adapt. I had the full support of my family and friends, which proved to be invaluable in the coming months and years.

I was soon to learn that you cannot have an ego as a sole parent. The ego has to go. A harsh lesson that you are not #1, not even #2 for that matter. Gone are the days when all you thought of was what you were doing, your job, your likes and what you chose to spend your time and money on and how you spent your time with your boyfriend, friends and having fun and getting the most out of life. Now your child is #1 - first and foremost, with your job second (to pay all the bills to support your child as you cannot count on your ex to provide any coin on the exact date each month, no matter what arrangements are made), then the house as third (as it is imperative that your child has a sense of security where they can retreat and call home, no matter what life throws at them).

Then last comes the magnificent sole parent (aka you) - the glue that holds their whole world together. But that's OK as you wouldn't have it any other way for now and this will change the older your child gets. My view is that your child will always be #1, no matter how old they become. I just had to take a leap of faith and give it my best shot. What other options were there? Have my daughter live with him fulltime? I don't fucking think so!

At worst - if I fucked up areas of the single parenting scenario, Cait might require some counselling at some point in her life. This I could live with. Better that, than remain in the relationship with my ex. If I exited now then the damage would be limited and contained. It was imperative that she was offered the best start in life from four vital areas: emotional, mental, physical and spiritual. That she was well-positioned to equip her to be able to cope with anything that was thrown at her in life and have the resilience to bounce back to the normal level and not fluctuate from high to lows of emotions.

Financially - I would have to adjust my financial position. Luckily enough, I had a great career and I earned good coin. I had my own company and I was very good at my job, but that additional wage from my ex wouldn't be coming into the equation anymore. That was OK, because he wouldn't be there to spend it either. So, it pretty much balanced out. I then sat down and prepared a list of incomings of my wage and all the outgoings, such as school fees, mortgage, utilities, food and general upkeep costs. I was good. Cait and I would survive on my income alone, even if he didn't pay any child support, and I would be able to manage financially. I know that I was fortunate in my financial position, but I knew that even if I wasn't, that I would still leave him. For me, nothing was worth staying in the current situation - even if leaving meant that I would have no job, no house, and no money and be on the bones of my arse. I didn't care. It would be worth it. I would simply move in with family or friends until I got back on my feet.

Luckily for me I still had my job. I bought a new house (albeit not as nice as the old one) but it was Cait's and mine. All I cared about was getting out of the relationship as quickly as possible and feeling joyful. I have quite a few friends who gave up great careers to have children, believing they would be in a marriage or relationship for life. You have an agreement that one of you goes out to work whilst the other stays at home and cares for the kids and house. But when you are faced with the decision of what you want out of the relationship, your logical mind automatically goes to "How am I going to survive"? The only funds you have are in the joint bank account with your partner, and most families or couples live week to week, so there is no reserve coin. No savings to be accessed. Most people are mortgaged up to their necks with the house, new car and other nice things that most families have nowadays. It is standard. So, then the panic of the control of the money comes into play. Your partner makes the coin and even if you kick them out or leave yourself, how the hell are you going to afford to live?

Here are some tips to help you feel more empowered and to get you back on track:

1. My grandmother gave me some good advice when I was younger. She said to have an emergency account "just in case". She said there is no greater fear than that of being trapped and feeling helpless in a relationship when you feel you are unable to leave because you have no money to run away with. She got that right! Try to put aside $20 a week and deposit it in a bank account (make sure the mail doesn't come to your house - use a post office box!) or give it to a friend to mind for you so that you have something to start afresh.

2. A friend of mine put coins and any spare cash in a metal tin and buried it under her rose bushes until she had enough to get out of the relationship. Her front yard was full of roses, oddly enough!

3. Buy gift vouchers from supermarkets when you buy your groceries and/or buy pre-paid visa cards and stock up on these. These won't be tracked by your partner and can be used at a later stage to buy the essentials such as food, clothing and pay for rent.

4. Buy things that can be hocked or pawned at a later stage - jewellery, for example. You may not get what you paid for them, but even if you get 50% of the value, it's better than nothing. All these actions are empowering and you will be very surprised how good it makes you feel to have this secret stash. When you encounter more and more unpleasantness from your partner, you need something to fall back on. Just knowing that you have some funds put aside will bring a smile to your face, albeit a secret smile to yourself, and will help make your situation just a little more bearable, for a little while longer.

5. Ask friends if you can do any paying jobs for them? Babysitting, maintain gardens, transcribing notes for people - anything to get some extra cash.
6. Sell household items on ebay or gumtree (Australia).
7. Community organisations can assist with rent, food and clothing for families. Do an internet search on money, help for people who want a divorce, free legal aid, and free counseling. You may be eligible for government assistance.
8. There is help out there, so swallow your pride. All you have to do is just ask for it from family and friends. People love helping another person; it makes them feel better. So, if they offer to assist, take them up on it. You would do the same for them, wouldn't you? Or you could pay it forward.
9. Get a part time job, whilst the kids are at school.

The key is to stay focused on your future. Don't look back. It's easy to get anxious, overwhelmed or scared about your decision. Think of a mantra that works for you. Mine was "I want more joy in my life". I even had these words tattooed in red ink on the inside of my left wrist as a constant reminder. Stay focused on what you what to achieve in life and be confident in the knowledge that you have made the right decision.

Get strength from other people who believe you have made the courageous decision to move forward in life - to close the door on your old life ...... and as you wait in the corridor of life until the next door opens, rejoice in the fact that you are a strong and amazing person. Everybody who I have spoken to have all said the same thing "If I can get through a relationship break-up, I can get through anything". It's true. You are stronger than you think.

After the initial assessment of being financially able to manage by myself, I felt a flicker of panic that I was the sole bread-winner for the house - that I was now responsible for absolutely everything! Fuck, fuckity fuck! I won't sugar coat it; an overwhelming sense of dread crept in. This sense of dread washed over me and caused me to panic on numerous occasions and resulted in many a sleepless night. I'd wake up in the middle of the night and think, "Fuck, what have I done?"

And then the rational side of me would talk my mind down and reassure me that it was all good. I would force myself to remember a particular ranting scenario that my ex used to play out, and I would take a few deep breaths and then say to myself that I had made the right decision. Then the panic and dread would fade away. The frequency of these events subsided over the years. But I won't lie - I did have my moments. You will most likely have them too, but have faith in your decision and keep reminding yourself why you walked away from the relationship.

On reflection, I am proud of what I had achieved. My daughter was happy, healthy, confident, caring, intelligent, compassionate and well-mannered (don't laugh - it's important to have manners. There's nothing worse than a rude child. Well, yes - a rude adult, I suppose).

I was financially able to pay for my daughter to go to a private school, have lots of holidays, have a comfortable home and not want for anything. Cait was always looked after, but never spoilt. She totally understands the value of money and now has a job of her own. But as all parents know, you will continue to help your child as you have unconditional love. Your child is the greatest view of all.

How to Exit

But how does one exit a relationship? Thinking about the right time and lining everything up to ask your partner to leave the house caused a lot of stress and many a sleepless night. Again, being a planner I executed the banishment perfectly. I had gone through all the pre-breakup activities and was confident that it was going to be alright. To set the scene, it was on New Year's Eve. I know, I know - it's a terrible day, but I needed to start my year with a fresh start, without him. So I organised for Cait to be looked after by friends for the day and night. I contacted my parents and brothers and gave them a heads up that I was going to ask him to leave that afternoon. My family was concerned for my welfare. They offered to park outside the house just in case anything happened and I might need extra support. I said 'no' and that I would be fine; that I would ring them when it was done. I had packed a bag for him with all his toiletries and clothes for a few days and put the bag in the spare bedroom.

I sat him down on the couch and said that we needed to talk. He wasn't that interested. I asked again, but in a firmer voice, emphasising that it was very important. He agreed and sat down next to me.

I remember it was a bright, sunny day and the sea breeze was blowing through the windows. I was nervous; I just wanted him out and the whole task done so that I could move on to face the consequences. I said that I wasn't happy and that I hadn't been happy for a very long time. He said that he had noticed that I was 'grumpy'.

I reminded him that I had tried over and over again to make it work and asked him to go to counselling which he totally dismissed as 'rubbish'.

I then said that I wanted a divorce and that I couldn't go on living with him anymore. I asked him to move out immediately. I said that I had packed a bag for him and that I would ring his parents to tell them that he would be moving in with them for the time being. I said that I would call him a cab to take him now and that he could come back tomorrow afternoon after I pick up Cait from her friends and we would tell her together.

He was in total shock. He just said, "OK. If that's how you feel".

He didn't put up a fight. He didn't ask me to take him back. He didn't say that he would change or asked me to give him one more chance - nothing.

So I got up and called a cab to take him to his parents' house. The second call was to his parents advising them that he was on his way and that he would explain why when he arrived. I got his bag from the spare bedroom and handed it to him. He still sat on the couch in shock.

The cab rocked up outside the house and honked its horn. He got up and I walked with him out to the cab and then walked away back into the garden and shut, and locked, the front gate.

I stood in the front garden listening to the cab driving off down the street. I closed my eyes and felt the sunshine on my face and the gentle sea breeze. I went into the house. The atmosphere and energy within the house had instantly changed. It felt lighter.

I called my parents and brothers to tell him I had done it. They were very relieved and asked if I wanted them to come over and sit with me. I said 'no, but thanks anyway'. I just wanted to enjoy the evening by myself and that I would call them in the morning.

I pottered about the house, watched a bit of TV and snuggled up to the dog on the couch.

I then got a fabulous bottle of French champagne out of the fridge, cracked it open and poured a glassful into my 'good' champagne glasses and said "happy new year" to myself, confident that I had made the right decision and that I would never feel that unhappy ever again.

I slept in the starfish position (in the middle of the bed) that night and had the best night's sleep I have had in over 10 years! I woke early and spent the morning packing all his items and put them in boxes. I also called a locksmith and got all the locks changed. This act cemented my decision that there was no going back.

The weeks and months that followed were hard and draining. He was still in disbelief as to what had happened. He was a very quiet man and internalised everything, which did not help the situation. He did write me a very long letter expressing his love and how sorry he was that it had come to this end. But it was too little, too late.

Exit Approaches

There are many approaches to take to exit a relationship. My favourite is the quick and relatively painless "Band Aid" approach. Being the practical woman that I am, I like to apply business methodology.

1. Go in prepared with a set agenda and outcome. Do not take a piece of paper with you (don't laugh - a friend of mine did this as he has a terrible memory and didn't want to forgot anything!) I would recommend you have a 'mental note' of what you wish to convey.
2. Apply some background to the conversation, then deliver the message and put forward recommendations or options.
3. Ensure that your tone is calm and your delivery is slow. I realise that you may be nervous in the delivery, but try to remain calm. You don't want to make matters worse. I can guarantee that your partner will not hear anything you have said after you relayed your message of 'it's over'.
4. I would suggest you conduct this meeting in a private place, and definitely not in a busy restaurant. Trust me, you don't

want the drama if the other party doesn't take the news well and makes a scene, which they are entitled to do if the relationship was meaningful.

5. Be honest as to why you are breaking up with them. Tell the truth, but remember that you once liked, or even loved, this person. It may be hard to recall why at this stage, but show compassion. Don't be brutal in your honesty. Apply the filter from the brain to the mouth. Words like "I realised I never really loved you" or "I'm not that attracted to you anymore" are too harsh. They may be true, but not appropriate.

6. Be sincere and try to intersperse the negatives with a positive or two. Imagine being on the receiving end of the conversation. Be kind to this person.

7. Treat the break-up like you are leaving your employment. You don't want to burn your bridges, and you never know who knows who out there. With social media being the way it is, you want to end on a relatively good note. You never know, you might need a reference down the track!

8. Don't slag off your partner as this may come back and bite you on the arse. Keep the details of the break-up to yourself. When asked, just say that you are better people and happier being apart. People don't need to know the particulars.

Be prepared for ..... well ...... for pretty much anything, really. Comments like, "I thought you were happy?", "Give me another chance", may come your way. Rehearse your responses to the questions/reactions you think your partner might say. The person may just walk off leaving you hanging. Or you may be subject to a tirade of verbal abuse as they are angry, combined with displays of uncontrollable crying and/or gut-wrenching sobbing (this is not gender specific).

If you have the luxury of time (by that I mean that they haven't slapped you across the face and stormed off), you may wish to communicate the next steps. Most people want a plan to adhere to. They might not like it, but you need actions and timeframes.

It is also imperative that you follow up the next day to see how they are travelling. You may not be game enough to do this directly, as they may not want anything to do with you at this stage. Perhaps you could contact one of their friends or family members to check in on them. This is the right thing to do. Tick, done, done.

SEVEN

....

DONT DISPAIR

On many, many occasions I despaired. I was so overwhelmed with everything that was going on around me, I couldn't see a way out. I began to flounder, panic, doubt myself, forget who I was, and forget my strengths and abilities.

Not only did I despair, but I was in pure disbelief at how my ex-partner behaved. His thinking was not logical in any way, shape or form. There were times when his behaviour was downright narcissistic. He projected such a concentrated stream of hatred and anger towards me that there was no logic to it. His ego was bruised - something that would make him feel inadequate.

I was at a loss to fathom what sort of logical mind would resent paying child support for the benefit of the child that we shared together. I'm convinced that he thought his hard-earned cash was being squandered for my own personal use and not for the purpose of paying for the welfare of our daughter.

He resented paying child support as he couldn't comprehend that his monthly payment only assisted, and didn't totally fund, the costs associated with paying for Cait's schooling, books, uniforms, sporting hobbies, food, clothing, medical expenses and a roof over her head. As your child gets older the costs increase substantially, especially for girls. School fees, school uniform, school books alone were cripplingly and child support payments do not cater for this.

He was trying to punish me for leaving him.

"Divorce isn't such a tragedy. A tragedy's staying in an unhappy marriage, teaching your children the wrong things about love. Nobody ever died of divorce."

– Jennifer Weiner, Fly Away Home

There will be days when everything goes wrong. There will be the constant bullying and harassment, nasty text messages, emails and stalking. The mental, emotional and physical exhaustion will kick in and you will not know how to carry on.

You can't help but to despair. Well don't - just don't .... it really does get better .... I promise.

Joyful example #1 - Look at your children (if you have them) and see the beauty and joy that they give you. Think to yourself: 'If I got nothing else out of the relationship, then I got my beautiful children'. This will bring a smile to your face. Love is all you have. Feed your soul with love for your children.

Joyful example #2 - You had the courage to remove yourself from the unhappy relationship. You are a truly magnificent human being. You have made one of the toughest decisions of your life. You decided that you were done; done with being unhappy and unfulfilled. You have demonstrated to yourself that you deserve better. You have shown your children that parents deserve to be happy and if a relationship isn't working, that you try and fix it, but when you get to a point after you have tried to fix it, and still it doesn't work, that you make the decision to split up, so that each person can be the best version of themselves they can be.

That children have a clear understanding of what a happy family should be. That arguing parents is not the norm and does not demonstrate how you should love.

Joyful example #3 - Take a deep breath in and then say this out loud "I will never be in that position ever again", then breathe out slowly. Repeat this three times.

Joyful example #4 - You get to explore and sleep with other people again. Yes, you should be shouting this from the hilltops!

When you are ready (and you will get there in your own sweet time), you get to experience the sensuality of new gorgeous bodies. You don't have to wake up to your ex-partner each morning with your first thought being "Why can't you just fuck off?"

Joyful example #5 - This is an opportune time to do some soul searching. Even though you might have chaos all around you, at the moment, and you have been to hell and back, take a minute to think how can I use this experience to my advantage? Are there areas in my life or personality that I could improve upon? Not for anybody else's benefit, but solely your own.

For example, for me there was a pattern in my work environment. I seem to attract narcissists and bipolar bosses. I guess I'm just lucky that way. Four of my last six bosses (I kid you not) have had the same 'unique' traits. Each worked in a different organisation. I'm not going to name any names here, but all four redirected me out of corporate life and onto to my true path. As painful as each nasty experience was, they all brought out sides of my character that had either been hidden for years or I didn't realise existed. I am pleased to say that two of the 'unique' individuals were discovered and they were dismissed from the respective companies. But corporations are great places for narcissists to hide, and in my experience, thrive. In each instance I grew stronger as a person. I learned to:

- Listen and absorb information.
- Evaluate that information and make informed decisions.
- Be true to myself.
- Speak my mind, in a calm and professional manner.
- Maintain my values and integrity.
- Support and stand up for what is right.
- Choose my battles. You may lose some battles, but you can still win the war!
- Identify the triggers that working for these sorts of people have on me and now know how to address and overcome them.
- Realise what emotions I felt when I interacted with each one.
- That human resource divisions ONLY work for the employer and not the employee.
- Learned how NOT to operate in an organisation.
- Some people are just not worth the effort.
- That shit floats to the top (aka management) with the exception of a few amazing people.
- Use the mantra an old friend told me once "in with anger, out with love".
- I will always be surrounded by people with different competency levels.
- That Teflon can be applied to the majority of the corporate drones as the shit that they cause just slides off and never sticks.
- Corporations love seagulls. A corporate seagull is someone that flies around and flaps their wings squawking, causing problems and then shits on those beneath them and flies away. My advice - don't give them a chip or feed them.
- A lot of people are just 'muppets'.

Two of these individuals were let go and one was actually physically escorted out of the building, which was a great delight to witness. I left two of the companies as it looked like the nasty pieces of work were not going to go anywhere and my emotional wellbeing was far more precious than a pay packet. I quickly found other employment.

I look back now and think because of them I meandered into my true calling. Without them (and some other unpleasant experiences) I wouldn't be writing this book, or any of my other books. I would have simply gone on my merry way, just existing and not truly living my life.

So whilst all your emotions are raw, think: is there is a pattern here that I have in relationships? Do I consistently choose the wrong person? Do these people have the same unique qualities? If you have a resounding 'yes' going off in your head, then the next logical step is to think why?

Why do you attract these people into your life? You need to break the pattern. To do this you need some assistance, whether that be speaking to a trained counsellor, neuro-linguistic programming (NLP) specialist or spiritual counsellor. Or perhaps reading articles that can provide assistance. Once you have identified the reasons why, then when you encounter the same traits in others, you will know the triggers, and more importantly, you now have the tools to address them, so that it doesn't happen again.

You gain your power back. You've broken the cycle and can start to attract more wonderful people into your life.

....

EIGHT

TIPS AND TRICKS PRE-BREAKUP

Music as a Saviour - Music helped me escape and drift off to another world. I immersed myself into all types of music from classical, opera, alternative, jazz, house and rock. I played music continuously to soothe and calm my soul from the pressures of each day spent with him. I would play Maria Callas', *Gianni Schicchi: O Mio Babbino Caro* and Torleif Theddeen's *Suite No1 in G Major for Solo Cello, BWV1007: 1, Prelude* and *Adagio in G Minor for Strings and Organ* by David Parry and the London Philharmonic Orchestra on a loop for hours on end. I frequented the opera and classical concerts to get my fix. I just needed to escape into a world that consisted of movement, joy and beauty.

I remember watching the movie *Love Actually* - it was the scene where the wife is listening to the Joni Mitchell's song *Both Sides Now*. I associated with that song and played it whilst driving to work in the morning when my marriage was at the end of its road.

Music also provided some much-needed messages that helped me to move on. I remember when we had split up and I bought my own place prior to settlement and moving, and I still felt so angry towards him. Somehow every time I turned on the radio or music video channels on TV, it always played the same song "*Wish You Well*" by Bernard Fanning ..... with the words "I just want to wish you well". I heard it everywhere.

I took it as a sign of how to interact with my ex. So, with any correspondence that I had with my ex, I responded with, "I wish you well" at the end of every conversation, text and email. It annoyed the fuck out of him. He couldn't work out if I was being sarcastic, bitchy or that I genuinely wished him well. Maybe it was all of the above, but it was liberating and turned the karma around - as if I wasn't buying into his negativity and abusive rantings. And it helped me.

Limit the Negativity that Surrounds you

With everything that was going around me during pre-breakup I was at my limit, and I was especially sensitive to any form of negativity. I identified those things around me that were upsetting or dragged me down (other than my husband). I disassociated with them. I stopped watching the news each night as I found it distressing. I couldn't bear the thought of watching TV shows or movies that were sad. So, no dramas, no thrillers or documentaries - only comedy. I needed to laugh and have joy in my everyday life. I stopped reading the newspapers and magazines. I would zone out when having a conversation with friends and work colleagues when they started speaking about world events. It wasn't that I was unsympathetic towards the plight of the world - it was simply too much for me to handle at that time. I couldn't cope with more drama! Everyday existence was all I could manage.

I culled friendships that weren't authentic. It was a radical and liberating process. I watched and observed friends and colleagues. If I felt the friendship was one-sided, then I just stopped being friends or I allowed a natural attrition to occur and they would simply no longer be in my life.

I was shedding, becoming lighter and not content to be dragged down by toxic and negative friends who drained the life out of me.

I trusted my inner knowing or 'my gut' feeling. The timing was right and I have never regretted my decisions.

Absorb Beauty

I sought beauty from wherever I could. It made me happy. I would visit the art gallery and drink in the paintings and sculptures. I regularly walked along the beach at night and watched the ocean crash against the shore. The wilder the weather, the better. Having the howling salt water bite at my cheeks would awaken my senses and power me on to face another day. I rejoiced in taking my daughter to the park and play on the swings, watching her squeal in delight as I pushed her higher and higher into the clouds as she said, "faster Mummy, faster Mummy". She was fearless. I noticed all nature around me - the ants walking in file to reach their destination and majestic old trees with strong protective branches. I had always had an appreciation of nature, but now I was focusing on the simple things in life to counteract the trauma that I was going through with the relationship.

Name change

I should never have taken his surname in the first place. But that was what was expected under the traditional marriage regime. I couldn't wait to change my name back to my maiden name. I have to admit that I did this in secret. As soon as it was legally possible, I went straight down to the local Registry Office and changed my married name back to my maiden name.

I felt instantly better and more myself. I was empowered. I would never have his surname again. I practised my signature over and over again. I lost count of how many times I signed my true name - Radford. The signature just flowed across the page. It was more flamboyant and captivated the very essence of me. I loved signing my signature.

The next step was swapping over my driving licence and passport photo and any bank account details that displayed my old name. It was exciting and it made me feel jubilant. You should see my driver's licence photo - I had the biggest smile! I was happy that I was getting back to my old self; pre wife self. A wonderful woman complete with her mojo - fearless and happy - and with the world at her feet. Perfect.

Light Bulb Moments

It's funny how different people come into your life at different times - to teach you a life lesson, make you feel that your life isn't that bad, or just to entertain or support you. Since my break-up I have met the most amazing people. Not that I didn't know some amazing people beforehand, but because I was opening up and becoming less guarded, more wonderful people were being attracted to me - people from all walks of life, with incredible wisdom and knowledge. I would be having a normal, animated conversation with one friend and they would come out with some absolute mind-blowing one liners that would stop me in my tracks and take me to the very essence of clarity, and I would think to myself, *Yes, you are right.* These one line statements are enough to have you stop, think, assess and make significant changes in your life. Bless those treasured friends who give you a light bulb moment! Most of the time they are completely unaware of what they have done or the impact that they have made in your life.

One particular dinner I was sharing with two old dear friends, and after a couple of grey goose caprioskas, we got onto the topic of ex-husbands and boyfriends. After recapping what we liked and didn't like about each other's ex-partners, both of my friends came out and said, "We are glad you split up with your ex-husband. We didn't really like him". It was shocking to hear this, but understandable, in hindsight. I never knew they felt like that - all I can say is that they hid it very well.

I have had many friends and family members and acquaintances who I have spoken to regarding the topics of my writing books and my business ventures. All have given invaluable suggestions that I have incorporated into not just my books and rapture business, but my everyday life. They are absolute pearls of wisdom that were given with love and generosity from dear friends wanting nothing else but for me to succeed in my venture. I thank them all.

Many light bulb friends come into your life to be the conduit between you and other people who can assist you in where you should be going in your life. If you lack direction and are wallowing in self-pity, then friends can lift you up, give you an idea and then steer you back on track again.

Amongst friends and family members providing surprising insight into your life and providing a different perspective, there are light bulb moments that shock you into waking up to the fact that your current situation isn't right. Being the stubborn woman that I am, it took quite a few of these moments for me to wake up.

One particular event was when I went to the doctors to sort out my left blocked ear. I took Cait with me after work to the local doctors to get my ear syringed with water. At that time I travelled a lot for work and being in a plane with a blocked ear caused immense pain. As I entered the doctor's room, I ran through what procedure I needed doing. The doctor asked me to sit on the top of a bed that was over 1m off the ground. She commenced syringing my left ear when I started to feel faint.

I advised her that I was feeling faint, but she ignored me and turned to fill the bowl with fresh water. The next thing I knew I was on the floor, blood everywhere, with the doctor shouting my name to wake up. I had fainted and dropped head first from the 1m high bed onto the concrete floor and broken my nose, busted my front teeth and scratched my face from my top lip up to the top of my nose. Cait was upset and sitting on the bed with a forlorn look on her face, sucking on a lollypop.

I managed to come around and learnt that the doctor had called for an ambulance to take me to the nearest hospital, as I had hit my head, amongst other things. With blood dripping down onto my white, silk blouse I was carted into the ambulance. The receptionist had tried to contact my then husband, but he didn't answer, so they contacted my next of kin - my Dad.

My Dad arrived pretty quickly as he only lived around the corner and looked after Cait for me. He then drove to my house to see if my husband was there. He was there - with his phone on silent. Dad picked up my husband and drove to the hospital.

As the injury didn't count as 'life threatening' I was placed on the bed in the emergency ward awaiting a doctor to come and look at me and conduct the relevant tests. My Dad had gone off to get some coffee for everyone.

Whilst laying on the bed with my lip split, nose broken, black eyes forming and blood everywhere, with my husband and young daughter standing next to my bed, I guess I must have looked like a battered wife. So much so that a woman walked past and looked at me and said, "you poor bitch", and then gave my husband the death stare. This was quickly followed by another woman's scowl (her bed had been wheeled and positioned next to mine).

I have to explain in detail what this woman looked like so you can grasp the sheer bizarreness of the situation. The woman had been in the shower and had started to feel faint, so she reached for the shower rose for support. But her weight had wrenched the 20cm diametre shower rose off the wall, and as she fell towards the wet floor her forehead managed to land on the shower rose, leaving a significant imprint of the shower rose on her forehead - complete with the circle and all the little water-spurting dots.

Engaging in a conversation with a woman who has an imprint embedded on her forehead, without bursting into fits of laughter, is a tough ask. I don't mean to sound callous, but it was rather comical.

So, the woman with the shower-rose imprinted forehead kept staring at me, only taking her gaze off me for a second to shoot daggers at my husband, who by this time was feeling extremely uncomfortable and excused himself and took Cait to get a drink and find my Dad.

Once he had left the room, the woman reached out and touched my arm and said, "I know how you feel, love. I've been there ..... men are all bastards! You need to get strong and just leave him - if not for the sake of yourself, but do it for your daughter".

I replied that my husband hadn't laid a finger on me (he wouldn't dare as he knew that he would be six feet under if that was the case) and that I had, in fact, had an accident at the doctors and fainted whilst getting my ear syringed and I was not a battered wife.

She replied in that patronising way, "It's alright, love. That's what we all say - they're all excuses. Don't worry - it will get better. Just leave the fucker before it's too late". With those parting words she was wheeled away.

I grabbed my handbag and found my makeup compact and looked at myself in the mirror. I looked like I had gone ten rounds with a professional boxer. My face was swollen and my eyes were very nearly closing from the bruising. My nose was obviously busted and broken and my lips looked like I had injected way too much collagen and looked like I had "trout pout". My new silk, white blouse was now my old blood-soaked blouse - it was completely drenched in blood. I did look like I had been beaten up.

I was seen by the doctors, had a head scan, got my nose stitched up and given painkillers and was sent home to rest. I had a couple of days off work to recuperate and relax. But during that time I reflected on the words that the shower rose lady said. I did want to get out. I wasn't happy and I felt like it was a message from the universe that this relationship wasn't right. I mean, it wouldn't even enter his mind to hit a woman - it wasn't that at all. It was more like, "You need to get strong and just leave him. If not for the sake of yourself, then do it for your daughter".

She was right. My life wasn't providing me with any source of joy. It was another light bulb moment.

Post Office Box

Getting a Post Office (PO) Box for my personal mail was more of a strategic move. Firstly, I already had a business for my company, so getting another PO Box for personal reasons was the next logical step. It only cost $20 per month at the time - a small price to pay for peace of mind. The main purpose of getting a PO Box is that if you are planning on leaving your partner it is essential that no correspondence be sent to your home address, so all your bank statements, lawyer's documents and private letters get posted to the PO Box. And vitally important, if you have changed your name back to your maiden name, as I had done.

It is also helpful in keeping control of your mail. A work colleague of mine had split with his girlfriend. The split was not amicable. His ex began to stalk him and as you can imagine it was very unnerving for him. One of things that he noticed is that he stopped getting any mail - not a bill, not any junk mail - not even a birthday card. We were having coffee together at work when he was telling me this story. He was rather perplexed, so he called the post office and they confirmed that the mailman had dropped mail off during the week - for the past four weeks, in fact! I suggested that he get a PO Box to monitor if was getting mail. It was possible that the mailman might not be dropping off the mail or that somebody could be stealing his mail. So he organised a PO Box and got all his mail redirected to his PO Box. Funnily enough, he started to get mail again. Turns out his ex-girlfriend was stealing his mail every day whilst he was at work - to get back at him. Not nice!

Change of address

Having a change of address brings up all kinds of possibilities. Are you planning on staying in the house where you currently reside? Or are you planning on finding a place to rent in the interim as you can't bear to be under the same roof as your partner? Or do you need space before you decide on the sale of the marital home? You really need to give careful consideration to all these possibilities. What would be your best or worst case scenario? The best is that your partner would leave. They would pay a percentage of the mortgage or rent until you have your financial settlement. The worst case is that you leave the home, and move into temporary residence or rent until everything is sorted. Do you want to buy a new home straight away? I recommend that you consult a family lawyer to get some answers to these questions.

For safety or legal reasons, are you OK with your ex-partner knowing where you are living? You might want to speak to your lawyer and ascertain if you need to disclose this information.

Professional Advice - Lawyer, Accountant and Counsellor

My motto is that it is always good to be prepared. When things are starting to go pear-shaped, you need to know what options are available to you so that you have all the information and can make the right decisions. Investing in professional advice can save you $1,000s (if not $100,000s) in the future. Not to mention the peace of mind it brings.

Lawyer - So, I contacted an old friend who had worked in the legal profession for over 20 years and asked her who was the best family lawyer in Perth. She advised the name of a law firm that was highly regarded. If things turned nasty then I wanted someone I could rely on and knew family law back to front and inside out.

Next, think about getting legal advice to ascertain where you stand with the split - both legally and financially. What are the next steps to do with the property, children, assets and liabilities? Do you need to lodge any documentation? These scenarios range from - the best scenario: both parties agree and you don't end up in court. The worst case scenario: you end up in court as neither party is willing to budge and it ends up costing you over $50,000 to $100,000 in lawyer fees. Not recommended, really. I mean, how many people have that sort of spare cash lying around? I would think that would be pretty much nobody!

I suggest you contact your local Law Society and ask for the names of three firms that deal with family law and then ring each of them up and interview them. Go with the one that feels right. Remember, they are working for you. Ask friends if they know of a good lawyer. How ruthless do you want your lawyer to be? Take note that these are only preliminary discussions, and that you are simply seeking a high level position on how you stand. If you can't afford a lawyer, do some research on the internet. Also, contact any free legal advice or citizens advice bureau or legal aid. The majority of lawyers that work for large firms do a percentage (albeit small) of providing legal advice pro bono (meaning free of charge). These lawyers volunteer their time.

You need to go prepared to the meeting. Have a checklist of things that you want to discuss as the lawyer charges in six-minute units and will generally charge AU $400-$1000 plus per hour for their time. Yes, that is the base rate of a good lawyer. Rates vary depending on seniority. In Australia you will need a solicitor for general advice and then if it goes to court you will need a barrister and they can charge thousands per day, in addition to your solicitor attending the hearing. Financially - it's not pretty.

Some things to consider prior to the meeting:

- Get a copy of all financial records for the period prior to coming together, during the relationship and post the relationship. This includes:
  - bank statements
  - superannuation statements
  - credit card statements
  - list of all share portfolio and current value
  - any business accounts that either party has
  - value of those businesses
  - trust funds for the kids
  - any trust funds or self-managed super funds

- Value of assets, such as:
  - cars
  - house (property)
  - boats
  - furniture
  - jewellery
  - artwork
  - toys (jet skis, surfboards etc)
  - tools (these are expensive)
- Ask what would be the best and worst case scenario?
- How would they think the assets would be split?
- What would be the timeline?
  - from now until you advise your partner you want to split
  - from splitting, ie from separation to divorce
  - how long will it take to finalise everything?
- Are you entitled to child support payments?
- Are you entitled to spousal support?

Take a notebook with you and write down as much information as possible. I can guarantee that you will forget some of the detail afterwards. Better still, take a family member or friend with you. Their interpretation may differ from yours. Do not be intimidated by the lawyer. Remember - THEY work for YOU. You are paying them (a lot) to be on your side. If you don't like the advice, then venture out and get a second or third opinion.

Accountants - In conjunction with getting legal advice, contact an accountant, so that you know where you stand financially. In more complex cases when you have a very creative ex-partner then you may need to engage a forensic accountant. These specialists are like a bloodhound. They can sniff money out from most overseas bank accounts and provide a complete audit trail of your partner's financial transactions. They are expensive, but if you have a gut feeling that your partner has more money 'somewhere' that you don't know about, then engaging the services of a forensic accountant will be worthwhile.

You will need to determine what your assets are (what you own) and liabilities (what you owe). Are you a director of any companies or trusts or superannuation schemes? Is your property in your name or your partner's name? Or both? How is your credit history? Did you ever miss any mortgage or loan payments? If you split, then will a bank lend you any money? Is it worthwhile setting up an account now with a different bank and getting your mail sent to your PO Box? Will you need a proven savings record? How long will it take to recover financially from your relationship?

Seek advice from your accountant and/or a financial planner on what you are to do post break-up. And get advice on how best to invest your money, if you emerge from the whole scenario with any (hopefully). Again, I would recommend that you get a few opinions from different experts. I know of too many friends who received bad advice and ended up losing everything in the global financial crash (GFC). And I mean houses, shares, cars and companies. They have had to start over again in their 40s and 50s and have never recovered. Not ideal. I would diversify your portfolio, with property, shares and fixed term deposits. Do what feels right for you. My first priority was to buy a new house for Cait and me. So, my money was invested in the family home. But you need to make your decision based on what feels right for you. My grandmother didn't trust banks at all after going through World War II, so she hid her money under her mattress, in her wardrobe and in various places around the house. I'm not saying do this, but go with what makes you feel comfortable.

Counsellor - After the simple, "there's nothing wrong with me, it must be you, so if you want to go to see a counsellor, then go" comment from my ex-husband, I did go and see a counsellor. Not for me (which, in hindsight, might not have been such a bad idea), but for my daughter. I asked what I could do to limit the damage to my daughter with the marriage break-up. How should I approach my daughter when we told her the news? What did I need to consider afterwards?

Here are some recommendations:

- The clear message was to support your child fully.
- Reinforce the fact that both her parents loved her unconditionally.
- That Mummy and Daddy had tried everything to make it work (yep, I know what you're thinking - this may be one-sided) but parents deserve to be happy and that they will be happier living apart.
- That your decision it is not their fault. Keep reinforcing this message.
- Keep the message simple, so that they are able to digest it.
- Don't blame the other party.
- Don't lie - kids know!
- Don't talk about the other party in front of them. Consistently say good things about the other party; how much they love them.
- Don't tell them any secrets as kids can't keep them. Plus, it puts them in an awkward position which makes them anxious and stressed, resulting in them withdrawing how they feel. You want how they feel to be openly communicated, even if you don't like what they come up with.
- Above all else, DO NOT USE YOUR CHILDREN AS PAWNS in the relationship. This is soul-destroying for ALL parties. Your children are innocent by-standers in this scenario.
- Discuss the next steps:
    - that your child will have two homes now.
    - that you will always be a family, but just live in different homes.
    - what will be the custodial arrangements? Week on/week off?
    - that they are the most important person in your life.

- keep the dialogue open all the time. The kids need to feel that they can tell you how they feel - if they are happy or unhappy.
- advise your child that it's OK to talk to another party to confide in - such as a grandparent, uncle, aunty, cousin or family member - preferably one who you trust and who is on your side of the family.

Strategies in place

- Gather all your information documents together - birth certificates, passports, money, marriage certificates and prized photos and give them to a trusted friend or family member who lives outside your family home. Just to be on the safe side. Just in case you need to run one day and you don't have time to pack.
- Do you have any witnesses to your partner's behaviour? If the behaviour is good, then you are OK. But if their behaviour differs behind closed doors, try to get some evidence of this as it may be needed in court one day.
- Do you have any character witnesses for yourself?
- Discuss the emotional, physical and spiritual impact that your relationship is having on you with trusted family and friends. Make an appointment to see a counsellor for expert advice on your situation.
- Meet with your doctor and discuss it with him/her. It needs to be documented that you attended if you aren't feeling well. Be careful that you partner doesn't use this against you to try and prove that you are emotionally and/or mentally unfit to care for your children, if you have any.
- Have a designated safe house. Ask a friend or family member if you can stay with them should 'the shit hit the fan'. I had a house to go to if I needed to crash for the night; if I just had had enough of him and needed to get out of the marital home for at least one night. Or even if I just couldn't bear it anymore and had a fight with him and told him what I

thought of him and walked out. I knew that I had a house I could go to. This was comforting. I think everybody has a house they crash at, if need be. I remember when I was younger and my flat-mates were getting too noisy and giving me the shits, I would go and park myself at my friend's house for a night to escape the circus.

Birth Control

The last thing I wanted in the final years of our relationship was another child. So I took myself off the traditional pill and got an implanon inserted in my arm (a slow release pill hormone). I didn't want to chance it. So, wear a condom at all times and remember - "no party, without a party hat". You don't want to be bringing another child into an already unhappy environment. Children are not bandaids to a relationship. I have yet to hear that a new baby brings warring couples back together. The stresses of a new child are enough to test the relationship of even a happy couple, let alone one that is heading to 'splitsville'.

Trust only a few

Tell your plans to only a trusted few. Do not talk to your children about your plans as they might 'spill the beans' to family members or, worst case scenario, to your partner. Talk to those who you can confide in, safe in the knowledge that what you say and do will not go any further. Ask for their advice - you may get a more balanced view of the situation, or they might suggest ways to help. I was surprised at what fonts of information my friends and family proved to be. If they didn't know about a particular topic, they knew of a good contact who most likely did know. Tap into the basic need that good people have. They want to help and be of service. Take people up on their offers of assistance, as one day you may well be asked to return the favour.

Support System

Get a support system in place BEFORE you split. Gather your possie of friends or family who will support you. Try to get a mixed bag of people. Friends who:

- You can just let go with and have fun, ie get drunk and dance with.
- Don't judge you (when you're smashed and dancing on tables or say horrible things about your partner).
- Who can provide a balanced view.
- Couples - you need a couple's perspective.
- Men friends who can provide a lot of insightful information.
- Who are strategic and sneaky. I know this sounds strange, but you need to have every angle covered so that there are no 'surprises'. So, if you happen to have some creatively minded friends who think differently, ask them what they think. What would they do in the same situation? If they split up with their partner, what would they do to them? The responses may shock you, but at least you will be prepared for the worst case scenarios that may eventuate.
- Who can listen and are available at unusual times. It may be in the middle of the night when you can't sleep, but you know you have friends in a different time zone who you are able to talk to.

Take a Snapshot of the Worst Moment

It is important that you remember the worst possible point in your relationship that you had with this partner. Think long and hard about how you felt, what emotions came up such as anger, heartache, sadness, frustration and betrayal. By having this mental snapshot of the worst moment you have experienced, will help post break-up, should you ever begin to doubt your decision. You can simply recall the snapshot and realise that you did make the right decision. Never again will you have to go through that experience. But you will use it as a turning point in your life and look back and be proud of what you have achieved and how far you have come since then. I guarantee this will bring a very big smile to your face.

Get Stronger

You need to get stronger - physically, emotionally, mentally and spiritually.

Physically - If you are not already physically fit, then start. I'm not talking about weight loss here - just having enough energy to get you through each day. Start walking, running, going to the gym, swimming - do whatever it takes, but just get moving. The benefits are four-fold:

1. You get fitter.
2. It clears your mind.
3. Endorphins (happy hormones) get released from your brain and make you feel better.
4. By being healthier, you will be able to cope better with the trying times ahead of you. Basically, you can't afford to be sick with the flu or any major illness during this time. You will have enough to deal with. You will no doubt be feeling stressed, so try and get some massages to release the tension or find a 'friend with benefits' to release that valve.

In conjunction with getting your body physically fitter, it's also important that you rest your body. Make it a goal to get as much sleep as possible. Sleep has amazing benefits to your wellbeing. It's similar to getting your car serviced. When you sleep your brain runs a check of your body and does a service of your body to keep it running in peak condition, preparing it for the next day. It is not only the quantity of sleep, but the quality, that provides the most benefits. You sleep in cycles, such as a deep sleep and

REM sleep. The deep sleep is when the body repairs itself, grows and boosts your immune system. Failure to get enough deep sleep will have you walking around like a zombie (aka the new baby phase when your baby wakes up every 1.5 hours like Cait did). REM sleep is critical for your brain function for memory and learning. During this sleep phase your brain processes all the information that you learned during the day and forms connections that strengthen the memory and replenishes the 'feel good' chemicals, like serotonin and dopamine that make you feel better. Basically, more sleep will give you a natural high and recharge your batteries to face another day.

Eating well is also very important as it fuels your body for the road ahead. Eat good food - organic if you can afford it. See a Naturopath and get your diet and supplements sorted. This will put you in peak physical condition. You will be a lean, mean fighting machine (if needed, that is).

Emotionally - If you are at the point of moving on from the relationship, chances are that you are already emotionally exhausted. Experiencing the rollercoaster of emotions plays havoc with your wellbeing. I'm emotionally very balanced and operate on a happy medium. So, I accepted that during this phase of my life, my feelings would reach the highest highs and the lowest lows. But this was OK, because it's called life. More importantly, however, I knew that it wouldn't last forever and I would gradually resume my natural state of being balanced.

Don't beat yourself up. Pat yourself on the back - you're doing a fantastic job. Who cares if you cry at the drop of a hat? So what? Do you feel better afterwards? Emotions have released. It's a very good thing.

I've rarely been one to cry. I'd watch sad movies and my friends would be reaching for the tissues and I'd be sitting there wondering, "What the fuck is wrong with them? It's not that sad!" I softened slightly after the birth of my daughter, but again

I didn't shed many tears - it just wasn't in my genetic makeup. After a discussion with a friend on the topic, she advised that I actually needed to release my emotions and get them out, as keeping them locked away would make me physically sick. So, she suggested the following:

- Watch the saddest movie you can find in private and see if you shed a tear.
- Whilst driving in the car by yourself, turn the music up and scream at the top of your lungs and release the anger and frustration.
- Dive into the ocean and scream underwater.
- Write everything down on paper about how you feel and then burn it and put the ashes in the soil outside in your garden.
- Do some physical activity, like boxing or play tennis and get your anger out that way.
- Go for a run and run as fast as you possibly can. This wasn't really an option for me as I have beautiful E cup sized breasts and the "girls" wouldn't appreciate bouncing around like that, unless they were having fun and got some reward from this type of activity ☺.

Mentally - Being mentally strong is hard to measure. What worked for me was having a simple goal to achieve. That was to get out of the relationship as quickly as possible with the least amount of damage to everyone involved. So, focusing on one goal can reset you if your mind becomes a magpie and gets easily distracted on some shiny new thing. Be disciplined in your approach with your mind. Let any worrying thoughts or noise go and don't focus on the negatives. Try and remain positive. Be the gatekeeper of your thoughts - your thoughts are your own. Think of your brain as a nightclub. Imagine you're the owner of this amazing nightclub, and you only allow the happy and productive thoughts to enter the nightclub (aka your brain). The negative, destructive and doubtful thoughts aren't allowed in. They can just fuck off and go to another club. They are not welcome.

I have a very active and complex mind. I find it a challenge to calm my mind for any length of time. I'm now practising meditation to see if this can make some difference. My version of meditation is sitting on the sand at the beautiful Trigg beach in Perth. I breathe in the fresh salt water air slowly, hold my breath and then slowly exhale, all the while keeping my eyes closed and feeling the sun on my face. I am barefoot and I dig my feet into the sand (fine sand doubles as a skin exfoliant). And I relax. I sit for at least 30 minutes each day to train my mind to be calm. It also helps that I am surrounded by pods of surfers in the ocean in front of me. It's an amazing juxtaposition of beauty. Then I walk back to my car to get my fix of humour as I witness the surfer's 'car park dance'. This dance involves the surfer standing at the rear of their cars as they wriggle out of their very tight wetsuits and dry themselves off with a towel, whilst trying to remain modest at all times. It's comical, to say the least. But you get to witness some very fit, toned and tanned bodies in the process. It's the simple things that bring joy into our lives, isn't it? ☺

Spiritually - If you are a spiritual person, then you may choose to turn to your preferred religion or delve deeper into spirituality. This could help you get through this period of your life and make you stronger. I'm not a religious person, but I am spiritual. So, you may seek guidance and gain strength from this, if it helps you. Regardless of your belief system, even if you don't follow any religion, you can believe in yourself.

....

NINE

TIPS AND TRICKS POST -BREAKUP

"When two people decide to get a divorce, it isn't a sign that they don't understand one another, but a sign that they have, at last, begun to"

– Helen Rowland

Stand **by your Decision.** Congratulations!! You did it - love your work. Now you have made the decision you need to stand by it and not go back on it. You can never go back now. If you start to waver, then remember the 'snapshot' of the worst day with your ex. So, accept responsibility for your decision, but don't beat yourself up, and show yourself compassion. You have been to hell and back - and survived.

Be Joyful!!

Smile and be happy that you are now single and in control of your life, do things that you always wanted and have some well-deserved fun. You have an amazing future ahead of you, filled with new hopes, exciting experiences and dreams. It's going to be fantastic.

Let your emotions out

Let's be honest here - the last few months (or years) have not been a walk in the park, have they? Therefore, you need to release all those emotions that you are feeling. It's normal to have lots of ups and downs, and feel an assortment of emotions, anger, sadness, confusion, fear, panic, hate and disgust. Letting your emotions out will heal your body and help you move past the relationship. It's important to acknowledge your emotions and vulnerability. Talk to your friends and family and communicate how you feel, so that you don't feel so alone. Your emotions and feelings may well be raw right now, leaving you feeling vulnerable. It's OK. This simply means that you are human. Rejoice in the fact that you can actually feel the full spectrum of emotions like any emotionally balanced person.

Stay Busy and Strong

I found keeping myself busy after the breakup worked a treat. This wasn't too hard to achieve what with working full time, running the household and caring for my daughter. And then add to that the legal, financial and practical items to take care of as a result of the relationship break-up. But by staying busy kept my mind off indulging in any negative thought patterns. Time goes by very quickly post break-up, which is a total contrast to when you were in the pre break-up space, where time drags on and even stands still. It's interesting that I had more of a zest for life after the break-up. With your newfound energy you may wish to focus on other things, other than yourself, such as volunteer work. Helping others will, in turn, make you feel better - helping out in a soup kitchen or aged-care facility, or you may choose to read stories to children at a library. That way you are giving back to the community and engaging with others.

Lay Low

When I conducted some research by asking male friends of mine what they did after a break-up with their respective partners, many answered that they kept a low profile for a while. It gave them time to process and work through the relationship that had ended. They didn't feel like going out and painting the town red ..... just yet. What I found interesting is that they applied the diving methodology of having a 'Buddy System'. One of their mates would come around and just hang out with them to make sure that they were travelling OK. It was like some unspoken 'blokey' code of conduct that their mate would need some company. That might involve watching TV, sport, playing the X-Box or just hanging and having pizza and beers. Then when they were ready, their mates would take them out and get them drunk and try to set them up with a date to get their confidence back, as being involved in a break-up had robbed them of their confidence and they needed to feel masculine again or just have their ego boosted.

With women, I find that they have a strong desire to lay low and absorb what has just happened in the relationship and ponder over how it got to be in such a bad state. Many focus on their health and try to keep occupied and at the same time dissect the relationship in detail to pinpoint the cause of the break-up and take any lessons learnt from the experience. In project management language, they conduct a post implementation review, covering topics such as, 'What went well? What didn't? How would you do things differently the next time you are in a relationship?' And so on.

From experience I have found that other areas of your life will also be in flux at the same time. Your relationship has ended, but you might be having issues in your workplace or family. Everything seems to come at once to test your resolve. The positive out of these events is to acknowledge that you are progressing and shifting in life. That the universe is forcing you to evolve as a person, building your character and moving you on to bigger and better things.

No contact with your Ex

This mainly applies if you don't have any children with your ex. I strongly recommend that you limit any form of communication with you ex. It doesn't matter who broke up with who, just don't do it. It's soul destroying as it brings up all the emotions all over again. I know some friends who have gone down this path of maintaining contact and it has ended very badly, and they have regretted the decision.

What led them to want to keep contact with their ex:

- They wanted to try and just be friends. I know this is hard and that you have broken up with someone who may well be your best friend. But before you even contemplate this idea, give yourself at least a six-month break. If you still feel the same, then approach with extreme caution. What do you seek to gain from keeping the contact? Most likely, there will be no sexual interaction. Think very clearly about your intentions. Do you have a morbid curiosity of what they are up to? Do you think that your ex will get back with you, if they see that you are different? That you are a different person now? Think about this for a second. Are you prepared to be friends with someone who broke your heart? If 'yes', then how are you going to feel when they start talking about their latest conquests? Will you be able to sit across from your ex and not think what a complete nasty piece of work they are?
- Wanted to reconcile with the ex. Really? Is this what you want? Your previous relationship didn't work for a reason. Have all these contributing factors gone? Have both parties resolved their differences? If 'no', then salvage some

self-respect and *just don't do it*. If they have, how do you know for sure that they have been resolved? If this is what you want, and as you are both adults and have free will, then good luck to you. If your relationship is 'repairable', then tread carefully with set boundaries and regular checkpoints. I wish you well.

- Wanted to sleep together again - OK, being a very sexual person I can understand and sympathise if your ex was an absolute knockout in the sack and you think that you may never get that satisfaction from another person. But if this is all that they had going for them, then it's not worth the hassle or the pain by going back with them - even for a quickie. From experience there will always be other people out there who will outshine your ex in the bedroom department ...... believe me. So get out there and start your sexual awakening and have fun discovering another suitable sexual partner.

If I didn't have my daughter I would never have spoken or communicated with my ex ever again. I would have dealt with all the legal and financial matters via my lawyer. But as we shared custody of my daughter, we had no option but to communicate to sort out pick up and drop off times, decisions concerning the house, finances, furniture, schooling - anything and everything. I did limit our communication with him as he just annoyed the fuck out of me, to be honest.

The post break-up was far from the 'bandaid' solution. It was not quick and painless. It was slow and painful. However, I did fully utilise my lawyer and asked them to put everything in writing, which helped me a great deal. What I did notice, however, was that when my ex came to pick up my daughter from my house, he never once looked me in the eyes. I think this was out of shame and/or guilt. Even when we caught up (at Cait's request) for her 18th birthday dinner, he avoided looking me in the eyes. I can only assume that he wasn't over the relationship.

Introducing a new partner to your ex

I haven't done this. I've had new partners but none of them have been introduced to my ex as he lives overseas and I really couldn't be bothered. But I distinctly remember being introduced to his new partner, and it didn't go down well. Firstly, he didn't provide me with any notice that she would be coming on the day. Secondly, she was on my property that I bought by myself, after starting again, after we split up. So this invasion of my personal space immediately got my back up. It was in the morning; I was running late for work, my hair was wet, and I had no makeup on. I have to admit that: a) I looked like shit; and b) I was so angry at being caught off guard.

So, from this experience I can only suggest that you try and plan it. Look your best at all times when you anticipate that you may run into ex-partners. If by some chance you run into them without any warning, then fake it and stand straight, and be very happy (even if you are dying inside) and SMILE. Just the simple act of smiling will automatically make your voice sound nicer. Even if it takes all your strength to not want to kill the smug fucker, fake it!! If nothing else, it will make the new partner think that you are at least pleasant. I know you probably don't give a shit about them, but deep down inside a very small part of you will want them to question why you split up .... that's all it takes ..... a simple seed of doubt.

Running into the ex-family members

This is a tricky one, as I have been running into my ex family members since day one. I mean it's not hard, given they live down the road and shop in the same suburb. Above all, I think it is best to apply the professional approach of being polite and courteous - of 'rising above it'.

Firstly, the saying 'blood is thicker than water', definitely applies as you are no longer an active member of your ex's family unit and they will undoubtedly side with your ex (whether your ex acted honourably or not). It's been over ten years since I split up with my ex, but only last year did I become aware that members of his family did not know the full story - only his version of events, much of which was sketchy to say the least. I always had a good friendship with his brother and had been good friends prior to meeting my ex. So when I ran into his brother at a restaurant last year, we sat down and had a good chat. I ran through my version of events about the marriage breakdown and the events thereafter (the majority of which, he was unaware). Whether he took what I had to say on board or not, it didn't really matter. What mattered was that I had given him a balanced view of events. I am sure that he would have discussed these with some of his family members. But the words that I said were all true, with no malice intended.

I had nothing to gain by telling him the truth except just that - I got to state my truth. I felt better, not just for me, but for Cait. I told him how disappointed I was that his family had little or no involvement with Cait. Following the divorce I can understand (but not agree) with them not wanting anything to do with me, but why should the same rule apply to Cait? She had done absolutely nothing wrong. She was and still is an innocent in this. Yet they stopped communicating with Cait, other than his parents would put a birthday and Christmas card with $50 enclosed in our letterbox every year. Not once did they knock on the door and ask after Cait. Not one of the other family members would contact Cait to ask how she was going or how she was feeling. Was there anything they could do? Would she like to go out on any of their family outings? Nothing. The only exception was her cousin "L" who kept in contact with Cait through Facebook, which was wonderful for Cait.

I think above all, this selfish act of exclusion by his family members is unfathomable and personally unforgiveable. Why would they deliberately hurt their own flesh and blood? I have always reinforced to Cait the same message - that my ex's family all love her very much. They just don't know how to express their feelings. I trust that this is true.

So some helpful hints to deal with ex family members:

- Look as good as you can whenever you go out. You just don't know whether you will run into them.
- Be polite and courteous.
- Smile and be happy (fake it, if needs be).
- If it helps as you smile, think to yourself, "you can all go and get fucked".
- Be confident.
- Keep your posture straight.
- When asked how you are, respond by saying that you are great, thanks, and that things are going really well.
- Ask them how they are, even if you don't care.
- Be careful what you tell him, as you know much of what you say will be relayed back to your ex. Especially be careful if you are going through legal proceedings as you do not want this interaction brought against you.
- End the interaction as soon as you can.
- Walk away with your head held high.

In addition to running into your ex family members, you will also have the issue of your own family members running into them. What your family says or does is really outside of your control. However, it may be worthwhile to speak to your family and friends beforehand and ask them to be civil and try to limit what they say and ask them not to provide too much information. Plus, they need to report back to you and let you know what was relayed.

Some family members get chatty when they are nervous and tend to overcompensate by divulging more information than they should. Others, like brothers, can think of nothing better than to tell your ex and/or his family what they really think of your ex. They don't, but they do have trouble biting their tongues, as they know that it would be worse for you and they don't want to add fuel to the fire. A friend of mine who is also divorced told me that her brother had run into her ex at a pub and had a confrontation with him. Harsh words were exchanged, tempers took over and they ended up in a brawl and got kicked out of the pub. As much as you may want to see your ex suffer, please be careful and just wish your ex well.

What to do with the engagement and wedding rings?

Well, you have a few options available to you:

1. Give them back - this exercise isn't really worth the effort to be honest, as this would mean communication with the ex. So don't bother. Refer to option 3 or 4.
2. Keep them - ask yourself why do you still want them? What do they represent? What purpose would they have in your life? Refer to option 3 or 4.
3. Melt them down and make new rings. I had a few rings - my wedding and engagement rings and my grandmother's ring. So I combined all the gold and melted the rings down into one rather chunky new ring. I asked the jeweller to embed the old diamonds, and added some new diamonds, into the gold ring. This ring now represents my journey. The engagement diamond represents my daughter Cait and then the other diamonds remind me of my grandmother. It doesn't remind me of my ex at all. I may give it to my daughter in the future.
4. Hock or pawn them for the money. If I hadn't gone with option 3, then option 4 (this option) is my preference. This has also been the preferred option of all the people to whom I have spoken.

5. Throw them away. I have heard varied stories from throwing the rings in the garbage, to the ocean, into lakes, rivers etc. This can be very therapeutic. But if you would like some coin, then I would go with option 4.

Wedding gifts

This is simple - you keep them. If you feel like being extra nice, then you can mention them in the property settlement and split them, if need be, taking care to identify which presents came from which side of the family. If the gifts are expensive (ie a house or car, etc) then you will need to consult your lawyer.

In laws (or outlaws)

It took a long time to be able to drive past the house of my ex in-laws without causing some kind of reaction. Now I feel nothing at all, but for a long time it wasn't like that. I would drive past and my shoulders would tense up and I would stress out thinking of all the times I had to put up with his family. The family celebrations .... Well, if you could call them that. It was always very awkward in my outlaw's house. Nobody relaxed - you could feel the tension as soon as you walked into the house. You know the feeling you get when you go into a family house that is filled with love, laughter, joy and memories? The place might not necessarily be tidy, but it's welcoming - like a warm embrace. You instantly feel right at home and feel that you can relax and just sit down on the couch and put your feet up. Well, his house wasn't like that. His family did try to be as welcoming as they could at the beginning of the relationship, but for the most part, there was an air of tension and awkwardness in that house.

I was never put in the position of having too many awkward encounters with the outlaws, as I very rarely engaged with them. At the beginning of the split I would ensure that Cait dropped off a present for Mother's (Grandmothers) and Father's (Grandfathers) day, together with a Christmas card. But sadly the relationship and the effort dwindled, so the visits became far and few between. I do think it is important to keep as much of the family relationships together as possible. I would like nothing more than for both sides of the family to get together and attend Cait's school events or witness major life milestones. But from the age of nine, my family attended the Grandfathers' or Grandmothers' day at school. Any school or sporting events were attended by my side of the family. The same applied to birthday parties and major milestones, like Cait getting her driver's licence. So, if you can bear it for the sake of your children, think about inviting your ex's family to milestone events in your child's life. They might not turn up, but at least you have done the right thing and offered.

Friends - Which side to choose?

It's not a pleasant thought to think that when your relationship breaks up that your friends have to make a decision to choose a side and stick with it. This is not a deliberate action, but a necessary one. I have yet to hear of friends who have successfully managed to stay friends with both parties. I hope I am wrong in this assumption.

Going into any relationship you will have your established friends and your partner will have their friends. So, naturally they will remain in your camp of friends post break-up. But what happens to the friends who you meet whilst you are a couple? Both individual friends and other couples. Well, a strange phenomenon happens in this situation. The individuals normally pick a side and stick with it. The couples, on the other hand, are in conflict. They have discussions about which partner they like more and make a decision based on that. What I found is that in most instances, couple friends will simply ditch both of the parties as they are uncomfortable being around either partner. This is due to:

- You are a reminder of what could happen if their relationship falters.
- Inviting you to dinner with other couples is awkward, like having an elephant in the room.
- They mistakenly think that you might run off with one of their partners and have an affair, as you are now single. I mean, really? As if!

So, I wouldn't take this course of action by your friends personally. I know you may be disappointed in their behaviour, but you have your current friends who you need right now and you will always make new ones in the future.

I experienced first-hand the "couple bypass" as I was ditched by what I thought was a great married couple. After the divorce I didn't hear from them for a good five years. Then out of the blue the woman in the relationship got in touch in with me and wanted to catch up. I agreed and we met up for a coffee. She mentioned that she had left her husband and she was looking for advice on what the next steps might be as "I had been through it already". I gave her as much information as I could, and she asked if we could remain friends.

I advised her that I was hurt by her, and her then husband's actions when I went through the divorce. She apologised and said it was just "too hard" to make a decision on which one of us they would side with as they only had couple friends. They couldn't agree who to side with, so they decided neither. I responded by saying that I would always be there to provide advice to her and support her, but I thought the friendship was damaged by her decision. I was true to my word and have directed her to lawyers, accountants and even babysat her children, but the friendship will never be the same again.

Living by Yourself

Once I had made the decision to not cohabitate with my ex-husband (basically when I asked him to leave our house), the euphoria of being on my own with my daughter finally hit.

I no longer had to adapt to his rituals and arrangements that dominated my life. Not that I adhered to his way of operating by any stretch of the imagination, like cleaning up after every single dish, vacuuming every single day and scrubbing the house from top to bottom. I actively rejoiced in doing the complete opposite to just annoy him. It was the simple pleasure of watching the vein at the side of his temple twitch and pulsate when I left one dish out overnight, on purpose. It made it all worthwhile.

I do not miss purchasing the mandatory six-pack of the best German beers that he liked to consume every night. It was extremely liberating walking around the house and not see his influence over anything. We very rarely agreed on anything in the house. We had polar opposites in taste of furnishings, furniture arrangements, colours, size of bed, food to eat - pretty much everything. The only commonality was that we both liked the best of everything.

So, even the simple act of food shopping after he was gone was joyous. I'd go up and down the food aisles and pick whatever food Cait and I fancied. Gone were the junk food items that he liked to consume on masse. One would think that he would be a large man, but 'no', he was blessed with a fast metabolism and was as slim as a whippet. Without the junk food, my grocery bill was far less and the food purchased was much healthier. I'd be walking down one aisle and I'd spot something that he loved and I'd laugh and gleefully think to myself that I never have to buy that food again, unless I want it.

The air of awkwardness was gone from the home. Our family home (Cait's and mine) is relaxed, welcoming, warm and inviting.

Friends and family dropped around more regularly. They didn't feel uptight and unwanted. I don't think my ex purposely meant to make friends and family feel this way, but I think he was shy, nervous and struggled with social communication with people who hadn't known him for years. This awkwardness oozed out of him and people misinterpreted this as not feeling welcome.

Living by yourself is very liberating. I enjoy the quiet and calm of my home. I had to train my brain to undo the methodical practices that I did each day with him. The mundane daily routine of what life is like when you live with a partner. You get to know their habits, their preferences, and their operating rhythm. By default, you start working with it. You entwine your rhythm to theirs subconsciously. You flow better as a couple or as team maybe. It's like a mutual unspoken agreement that you develop between you. But when you break up, you now have to remember what your rhythm was like before you met them? What did I do? How did I use my time? What was I like as a person?

You try to recall as much of your pre-relationship self as you can. One thing that I did remember is that I really enjoyed reading the paper on a Sunday morning outside. I used to pour tea into a beautiful ornate turquoise teapot and then put a china cup and saucer and milk jug on tray; then park myself outside on the day bed and read the paper at a luxuriously slow pace, whilst sipping my freshly brewed tea. I recall I used to think it was so decadent at the time, not having to rush. I could afford the time to sit down, relax and read what I wanted to read. Drinking from a china cup represented the weekend or holidays. During the week I used a mug as this was quick and easy and I normally drank coffee. But the weekends were special and a time for relaxation and unwinding.

The only downside that I felt to living by myself was that wherever I looked there was sole responsibility. I was responsible for running the house, which wasn't new to me as, I had always done that. But paying the mortgage, all the bills, putting the garbage bins out every week, changing the light bulbs, maintaining the house, being the one in charge of getting up in the middle of the night if anything went 'bump' (all of which I did as a married woman). Probably what I missed (not that I wanted it with my ex) was companionship and having someone to make me a cup each, whilst they were up. The latter (making tea) I addressed by teaching Cait and it became one of her jobs to do around the house and she became very accomplished - practice makes perfect! The companionship side was addressed by having male friends and partners.

The best thing was that the house was all mine and Cait's. It was our family home - the family that now consisted of Cait, me and the two dogs. My family members had keys to the house, so if they ever needed a break or wanted to drop in, they could. Friends were always welcome and I always had a spare bed made up for them to crash, without question or judgement as to why they needed the bed. The fridge and pantry were always stocked with great food and drink. The home was warm, welcoming, comforting, open and full of life and beautiful energy.

I would often drive in the driveway and stay sitting in the car and just pause for a moment and look around and absorb just how far I had come and congratulate myself that I had done OK, my grandparents' voices ringing in my head saying, "you've done alright, kid". I was truly blessed and grateful for everything. Cait and I had survived – we were happy, healthy, loved and above all, we felt rapturous joy.

Home Maintenance

Some may scoff at this topic, but it is a very real issue for most divorced (and single) people out there - in particular, women. You have three options available to you.

1. Outsource - if you can afford it. Do some research and ask as many people as possible if they know of any good home maintenance people who can help with things you don't know how to do. Definitely get the specialists in for plumbing and electrical work. The house is your biggest financial asset, so take care of it and maintain it.

2. Do the jobs yourself. Learn new skills. You will be surprised at how much you can actually achieve when you set your mind to it. I learned how to paint walls, patch walls with plaster, fix the pool pump, test the chlorine and salt levels of the pool, change light bulbs, change a tyre, replace spark plugs, fix broken fly screens, tend the garden (not my favourite activity), change sprinklers, lay pavers, drill a hole in the wall to hang a picture (knowing which drill bit to use for brick and plaster walls), use the gap filler, and replace roof tiles.

   Many friends of mine (both male and female) have taught themselves how to tile floors and walls, renovate bathrooms, laundries and kitchens, build walls, concrete posts in for fencing, and pave. There are even courses that are run by local warehouses that teach you how to do these successfully. I also use YouTube, as the instructions are great. Go to them as they are free and you can skill up. Not only are you learning and getting enjoyment from achieving this, but it is more cost effective.

3. Do nothing - not recommended. As I said in item 1, your home is your biggest financial asset and you need to protect it. You don't want your house to lose its value. Or worse still, if your house is not properly maintained and you decide to sell it, then you would most likely not get the price you want, in which case you would need to do a LOT of maintenance work to finish it to an acceptable standard so that it's 'sellable' to the buyer. It's far less costlier to you in the long run if you keep an eye on your house and tend to maintenance issues as they arise.

One thing to note is that a lot of my female friends are often unsure about a tradesperson coming through the house. Some think that they could be overcharged, feel unsafe (like the tradesperson knows they are alone and could be casing the house) and/or they talk to them like they are stupid and are just the "little woman". I have been lucky, I guess, and hold my own when engaged with tradespeople. Here are some tips:

- Don't discuss your marital situation with them, as it's none of their business.
- Do your research prior to the tradesperson coming to your house.
- Advise that you will be getting a few estimates from other suppliers so that it keeps them competitive.

A good friend of mine recommended that I list some suggestions below when dealing with people coming to your house for quotes and/or doing work for safety purposes.

- Leave a pair of men's work boots out the front of the house, so it looks like a man lives at the house.
- Put a wedding ring on the left hand ring finger, so that you appear married to the tradesperson.
- Say that you have a partner, but that you make all the decisions.

For those with Children

Parent Teacher Evenings - If you have children, then 'yes', you will no doubt need to attend Parent/Teacher evenings at your child's school. Regardless whether you work or not, book the meeting after hours. Turn up in business attire and look like you mean business. Don't go into any details about your private life or your child's home life. I can guarantee every teacher knows your "situation" already, especially if it's a Catholic or Anglican school. Walk with your head held high. Take the comments about your child on board, make the meeting as quick or as long as you want. Rush in and rush out as if you are very busy and your time is valuable. Don't hang around with the other parents, as it just gets too uncomfortable.

It's interesting that when you're married you don't really notice people's wedding rings. You are part of a married club. But as soon as you are separated or divorced, it's the first thing that you look at. All the married women stay with their husbands at the parent teacher evenings. They stick to their husbands like glue, as if the separated or divorced women will swoop in and grab their husbands. They are fiercely protective, as if they have a precious jewel that they don't want to let go. All the married couples stay together in a pack and then move as a pack. They'll ask how you are going and if you have met that 'special' someone yet. Apparently, you are a threat. Seriously? I mean, look at their husbands for starters. Who would be bothered? Give me some credit - I'm not desperate. Then the husbands get pulled this way and that, not even allowed to talk to you.

I'm an outgoing confident woman with a warm and engaging smile. In my profession I work in mostly male-dominated industries, such as mining, oil, utilities, to name a few. I've worked with men throughout my career, and I prefer to work with men than women. I love cars. I'm interested in how things work; I'm interested in politics, engineering, politics and sport, and have been blessed with being able to talk to anyone about anything. So talking to these guys is not hard. I can find something in common with anybody. But no, they are not allowed to converse with a single predator that has the potential to whisk them away from the family life. What was worse is that I worked and knew a few of fathers at work. So, the fact that the wives moved them on was very offensive as I respect the sanctuary of a happy marriage. I wouldn't like to be cheated on. I think it's great that people are married. My parents have been happily married for nearly 47 years. Hats off to them!

So, attend the function. Be strong and confident, and talk to whoever you like. Look as perfectly put together as you can, and smile and be happy. You have wonderful children - be thankful that they are healthy and they are yours. Plenty of reasons to smile.

School Events - Not sure about what country you are from, but here in Australia we have this school driveway etiquette called 'kiss and ride', where you drive up the school driveway in your car and drop your kid off at the school entrance with a kiss. Then you drive off. It's one of the best inventions ever, I think. There are two type of mums at the schools. The ones who work (ie me) and the ones who don't. So, the kiss and ride functionality is a life saver. You drop the kids off and at this point you are normally running late, your makeup isn't done and your hair is a mess. You have just spent the last hour stressing to get your child out of bed, have some form of breakfast and get them dressed for school. At the last minute you are informed of various forms that you need to sign, and that they need money for some event or the other. So, you're in a mad rush to do the minimum to yourself to get them in the car and to school on time so that they don't get into trouble.

Funnily enough, Cait was always late - no matter what time we got up. Cait had one speed which was commonly known as 'Cait time'. She couldn't be rushed, no matter what. She had to do her tasks at the same pace, and all the time you are thinking on the journey to school about the traffic on the freeway and how you are going to be late for work. But having a child at school is like being back at school yourself. I've never met such a group of judgmental people in my life. It's like high school. Nothing goes unnoticed. The car you drive, the food you give your child for lunch, where you live, what you do, who you know and your marital status. It's all noted!

School Sporting events - Be very prepared the night before with all your food, drinks, chair, blanket, ipod and headphones and book and arrive at the school venue early. Find a shady spot under a nice tree and mark your territory. Put your chair up and place your picnic rug out in front of you (the bigger the rug the better!) as this will provide a buffer between you and the other parents. I bring all the food in an esky (cooler bag). Not only does it keep the food and drink cold, but I can also put my feet up on it and use it as an ottoman. Once set up, put your hat and sunglasses on and put your earphones in and start reading your book. This ensures that (most other) parents won't engage in conversation with you for a while.

Next is the food. When the kids have a recess break, they are normally allowed to sit with their parents. So, be prepared for a group of kids to come and join your child on the rug - this is where the good food comes into play. You have to ensure you have good quality food and a lot of variety. Ideally, a fruit platter (that you bought the night before pre-cut), fresh juices, great bread rolls with interesting fillings, then some fun stuff like lollies (candy or sweets) if need be, but natural, of course. Little or no junk food as this will be noted and reported back to the "unworking mother's mafia". At the end of the day you pack up quickly and get out of there before you are volunteered to take down the marquees.

I found that other working parents did contact other working parents the night before asking if I was going and because they were working could their son/daughter sit with Cait and me. I always said 'yes', as the working parents have to stick together.

School Canteen duty - This is simple - just don't do it. Try and volunteer in the classroom for half a day or on a sports day. The last thing you need is to be judged on your culinary skills in prepping all the food. Then what's worse is dealing with other people's kids and serving them food. Trust me, other people's young kids are not cute or charming. They are demanding, picky, never have the right amount of money (basically they are always short) so you end up feeling sorry for them and footing the bill.

Then the worst ones are the ones who are allergic to something and ask if the orange juice has peanuts in it. I mean, come on!!! Be it at our own peril, if you do choose canteen duty.

Volunteering in class - As I've said in Canteen duty, if you have a choice then do the volunteering at class rather, than the canteen. But if you can't avoid it then limit your involvement. I managed to survive seven years of primary school with just two sessions - one when Cait was in Year 1 and I assisted in the computer room for a morning. And then again in Year 3 when the kids were making scarecrows. My suggestion is that you try to limit the sessions. You'll no doubt get questions from the teachers about how you are travelling, knowing full well it is all being reported back to the rest of the teachers in the staff room at lunch time.

Birthday parties - I realise that the ex-partner wants to be involved in the birthday parties. Here, you have two options:

1 – have separate parties for the kids and the friends/family

2 – combine them.

I recommend the first option - you can control the environment and the outcome of the birthday party, and the ex-partner may well see this as the ideal time to sabotage the event with their own personal grievances, as was the case with my ex. My daughter was upset that he was there as he was rude to the kids and never smiled or mucked around with them. So if your ex cannot be civilized, hold your own party with your child's friends and then your party with family. Then when it's your ex's turn they can do the same. I sold it as the 'festival of Cait', so she had a whole week and two weekends of birthday celebrations. Kids love presents and parties so it was a win, win.

Christmas and Easter - Where do I begin, really, on this one? Possible options are to take it in turns per year or split the day. In my case I split the day as I simply could not bear the thought of not seeing my baby on Christmas Day - it would have broken my heart. So, it came down to either the morning with me up to lunch time, and then the afternoon with him. That way my daughter got the best of both worlds and got to have two dinners and two lots of attention and presents. But as I'm a bit selfish, I prefer the mornings as I have a traditional routine that I do every Christmas. Even though Cait is at the amazing age of 20 years, I still wrap up her presents and put them in her room at night time, so when she wakes up in the morning they are at the bottom of her bed - lots of parcels. She wakes up and comes and gets me and we go back to her room with the dog and cat and open the presents together. She loves it. I don't think she will ever outgrow this ritual. I love nothing more than seeing her face light up when she opens each present. I have all different size boxes for her and her room is a mess afterwards. But it's the fun part of ripping the paper. She always lines her presents up in a row afterwards and reassesses each one. I am a very good present giver.

Drop off and Pick up - I have numerous friends who have this issue. The general consensus is to have a neutral place to do the kids drop offs/pick ups. Whether that is the local school car park or shopping centre car park near a fast food outlet or bank, it needs to be a place that is open, has witnesses and cameras (just in case). In addition to this you will need to have a witness of your own and above all bite your tongue. *I cannot emphasise this enough.* I had one friend whose ex-partner used to bait her deliberately and then he'd get his friend to film her on a video recorder, which he then later used in court to say that she was an "unfit mother". So, go with a friend in a neutral place and drop off the kids. Also keep a diary and write down the times and dates and any communications that you have with that ex-partner.

New Partner - This has to be handled with complete diplomatic caution. Do the right thing and introduce your child to your partner once you are certain that your new partner is a 'keeper' and will be in your life for a while. And that you are sure they are a good person and meet as much entry criteria as possible. Give your child some time to get to know the new partner. These things cannot be rushed. Talk to your child and say that this new partner is not replacing the mother / father as they already have one of those. But that this new partner makes you happy and is important to you and that you would like for both to get along. After the first meeting check in with your child (alone) to hear their thoughts. Again, take it slowly. Your child might be on board straight away, or it might take years. It's important to note that when you are out with your new partner and child, that you give them both attention. I have heard too many stories about new partners thinking that they are competing with the children of the new partner for attention and feel jealous. Yes, I know this may sound ridiculous, but it does happen.

Please do not do what my ex-husband did to my daughter. He managed to meet a new partner and proceeded to get her pregnant. Then he made the decision to travel to the UK and marry her overseas. This is major stuff, but he did all this without telling my daughter or inviting her to the wedding. She found out when her new stepmother posted a picture of herself on Facebook in her wedding dress (complete with large pregnant stomach) with my ex-husband. My daughter was devastated and disgusted. Real nice move there, Mr Father of the Year!

School Ball/Prom - I have to admit the only reason I bought my old house was for the grand staircase. Well, maybe not the whole reason, but it played a major part. I envisaged my daughter walking down the staircase in her ball gown, looking beautiful. And she did. She looked amazing - it took my breath away. My baby girl all dressed up, hair and makeup done. It was a knock out dress. I couldn't be happier.

My ex didn't witness this 'once in a lifetime' event, because he was living interstate at the time. But if you are on good terms with your ex then I would invite them to experience the coming of age of your child on this momentous occasion. I would limit the time period though - arrive at a certain time, have the photos with your child, and then celebrate with a couple of drinks. When the event is over, your child hops into the limousine and it's all very clean and civil - no dramas. You don't want any uncomfortable chatter afterwards. I would recommend that only your ex attend and not the whole family, as you don't want to get into any discussions about - well, anything really!

What do your kids' friends call you? - What do your kids' friends call you when you have changed your name back to your maiden name? This would depend on how formal your communication is with your child's friends. Strangely enough I have always been called "Mrs Caitlin" by Cait's friends, which is very cute, I think. This is neutral territory for both child and adult and is still respectful with the "Mrs", yet informal with the "Caitlin" as they do not wish to offend on the surname front as many mothers keep their maiden name.

The older that Cait becomes, so the formality has changed, I think. I am now referred to by my first name as "Gaina" by her boyfriend. Ultimately, you can choose which name works for you, but you will need to be consistent as your child's friends will use this name when they are still in their 20s.

Holidays - Holidays can be a very difficult and trying time for all, especially when you have joint custody of the children. I would strongly urge both parties to sort these arrangements during the court case or if you split on good terms, put the holiday plans in writing. It would be beneficial to include in the court orders to get agreement on:

- The notice period that each party has to provide to the other party when planning holidays.
- Document the approval turnaround time for each party to get back to approve the holiday time period. An example being if the mother wishes to take the child on holiday to Europe and

wishes to buy the cheaper prices for the tickets. Then the mother would prefer to provide as much notice as possible. When this request comes through then the father has 48 hours to approve. If the father doesn't get back to the mother during this time period, then it should be taken as approved.

- Passport application to be signed and approved by both parents.
- Overseas arrangements to be mutually agreed upon. One partner is not allowed to take the child out of the country without the other parent knowing. This would then address any concerns of possible kidnapping and taking the child overseas.
- That the handover for the holiday is on neutral territory.
- That the child is able to contact the other parent during the holding when he/she requests it.

I was in the fortunate position that my ex lived interstate, which meant that the holidays were very well-organised. Cait was flown by the lovely Qantas Airlines as an 'unaccompanied child" during the school holidays. I would hand Cait over to the Qantas staff and then they would take care of her on the flight, then my ex would pick her up from the same airline staff in Melbourne. The visits would go for a block period of time - normally a week.

But I have heard too many stories of holiday arrangements going awry, where one partner organises a holiday with the kids and then the other partner will say 'no' a few days before, resulting in the holiday being cancelled. But who loses out? The kids lose out in this scenario. Holidays are mostly looked back upon with happy memories, so get agreement as much as possible during the court hearings to ensure your holidays are the happy, fun-filled events they are meant to be.

Using the children as pawns in the relationship - To all parents of this world, I want to make it very clear - please do not use your children as pawns in your relationship. There are no winners in this scenario - everybody loses. I have always spoken well of my ex in front of my daughter. I continuously reinforce how much he and his family love her - because this is the truth.

Unfortunately, too many couples use their child/children as pawns in the relationship breakdown and post-divorce. This emotional tug of war between the parents is damaging to the child. Many questions get asked of the child that put the child in a very awkward and untenable position:

- What did your mother/father do this weekend?
- What food did you get fed?
- What time did you go to bed?
- Did you have a bath/shower?
- Did Mum/Dad get angry with you?
- Does Mum/Dad spend time with you?
- Did your Mum/Dad have any visitors this weekend?
- Is Mum/Dad happy?

The parents' feelings get projected onto the child, as if the child hasn't got enough to contend with. Parents have been known to turn their child against the other parent as an act of revenge. What is this teaching child? What warped life lessons are learned here? The child has been told by the parent to keep secrets, to lie and not give any information to the other parent. This is very damaging for the child as they are very fragile and not emotionally mature enough to process or understand the adult dealings. This can lead to the child growing up to suffer from low self-esteem, depression, anxiety, have trust issues and overall have a very jaded view of what a relationship and friendship is all about. So, how do you help your child?

- Don't speak ill or blame your ex-partner.

- Don't argue with your ex in front of your child. Try (if you can) to speak amicably with each other for the benefit of your child.
- No secrets to be kept by the child. Let them communicate openly and honestly without punishment, even if you don't like the answer they give.
- Take the time to listen and understand them. Get down to their level and speak to them about their day. Ask them how they are feeling and if they are worried about anything. I have found one common medical problem that young children suffer is stress. When the child feels stressed they tend to have pains in their stomach from the tummy muscles cramping due to not going to the toilet. Stress can cause constipation in some children (and adults for that matter).
- Have fun with your child and let them know that you love them unconditionally.
- Reinforce to them that the divorce is not their fault.
- Hug and kiss them every day.
- Ask your other family members and friends to keep an eye out for them - ie let your child know that they can talk to other members of the family if they don't want to talk to you about it.
- Get them a pet. I know this might sound a bit drastic, but kids talk to their pets about everything. The pet loves them unconditionally and the simple act of them stroking and talking to the pet can help.
- Check in on your child a lot to ensure that they are travelling OK.
- Provide an outlet for their frustrations, such as a sport or other activity. Like adults, children need a physical release for their emotions so they don't get bottled up. Book your child into swimming, basketball, netball, soccer or running.
- Provide as much 'kid time' as possible so that they can just enjoying being a kid. Have a look at the inner child section of this book for some suggestions on what you can do together.

Dating - Your kids involvement - I have to admit that I do not understand why people on dating sites have pictures of themselves that includes their children. It's a dating site, and not Facebook. Why the hell do they do this? Is it to prove that they love their kids? That they can commit to something? Or make them look like a great parent? I understand that they love their children, being a mother myself, but there is no way I would put the privacy of my child at risk by having pictures of her on a dating website with me. There are a lot a weird people out there and I do not want them looking at any photos of my daughter. So, if you plan on being on a dating site, clearly state that you have children, but do not put photos of your children on the site.

I think that I am more cautious and protective than some parents. I have to be so sure that the person I meet is the right one before I introduce him to my daughter. This can take months before I introduce them to each other. Cait is aware of the men that I see as we are very open with each other, but I know that Cait doesn't want to witness a string of men coming into my home to meet with me. Show some respect for your child as the house is their family home. Then once you are comfortable with your new partner (and you have, of course, communicated that you have children), by all means introduce them to your new partner. Your child plays a pivotal role in your life and their opinion of your new partner matters.

TEN

....

REDISCOVERING YOUR INNER GODDESS/GOD

I believe that rediscovering your inner goddess or god is essential ... but it may take time to bring this to fruition. It's a long and gradual process and requires time and effort. You will also need to be in the right head space for this glorious embrace. People can give you many compliments, but you just won't believe what they say to you until your self-belief is nourished and grows. Until then, it's pretty fair to assume that the last thing you will be thinking about is your inner goddess/god - it just won't be on your radar.

I don't think it's too far off the mark to say that your heart and soul is brutalised by the events of the relationship dissolving. You may encounter chaos all around you. What you now need is to find some calm and be soothed.

On conducting some quite extensive research, and regardless of gender, I found a few common denominators that people experience post relationship break-up:

- Their confidence was non-existent.
- They didn't feel attractive.
- Too tired by the whole experience.
- Felt jaded.
- Wasn't ready to meet anybody 'worthwhile' just yet.
- Would like some fun, but nothing serious.

- Self-doubt about their bodies.
- Didn't have time to invest in themselves with work, kids, going to court (if divorce proceedings still in progress).
- Weren't aware of who their 'inner God/Goddess' was before they got into a relationship, so how the hell were they expected to find it now?
- It would all be too hard.
- Required too much effort.
- Does it really matter??
- Couldn't afford to pay for 'massages', if that's what it means to find your inner goddess.
- What's in it for me?
- I go to the gym - isn't that enough?
- That's too 'airy-fairy' for my liking.

Physically

You need to know and love the body that you're in. Clothes are the first thing to consider, regardless of gender. You know what suits you and what doesn't by now. If you don't know then you may need to ask your family and friends, "What do I look good in?" Or visit a professional stylist. Regardless of what size you are, assess your wardrobe and throw out clothes that you never wear. Throw out the clothes that you 'might just fit into one day'. These clothes serve no purpose and are not your friend, as you get upset when you see the sight of them each time you venture into your wardrobe.

Throw out any clothes that belonged to your ex. Do not keep any clothes that smell or remind you of them. Remember, this is a clean start.

Toss out any clothes that you wouldn't wear into the city. Keep some clothes that are smart casual and then clothes that you can work around the house in and/or paint in. Do not go to the local shops in your 'work around the house' clothes. If you have the money, buy some new clothes that suit your shape that are flattering to your size, height and are age appropriate. The term "mutton dressed up as lamb" must not come into this clothing equation. If you're unsure of a particular item of clothing, ask a friend, "Do I look like mutton dressed up as lamb in this?"

You have one body. It's not going anywhere, and by now you should be aware of your body's limitations. What it is and what it can and cannot achieve - for now at least.

So stop what you are doing and go to your bathroom and, if you please, do the following exercise for me. Basically, strip naked and stand in front of a full length mirror and take a good, hard look at yourself. I mean it - it's important.

Notice the parts of your body that you like first ...... and before you say it ..... yes, you do have parts that you like - whether they are your eyes, ears, feet, breasts, arms, legs or stomach.

Then grab some body moisturising cream and start to massage it into your body slowly, taking time to notice how the cream is absorbed into your skin. Take note of every pore, hair, freckle, mole, marking or scar. Your skin is truly amazing and protects your body in many ways. As you massage each square centimetre of your body, reflect on the joy your body has given you over the years. Your lips have felt the tenderness of your first love's kiss; your fingers and hands have stroked tears away; your arms have held and comforted many; and your legs have allowed you to jump for joy and support your body's purposeful walk.

You may find yourself stopping at areas of your body that you don't like and instinctively skipping over them. There'll be no skipping over these areas, OK? Go back and lovingly rub cream into them too. What do these areas represent? How do you feel when this particular part of your body is touched? Why skip it? Doesn't it deserve to be loved like the rest of the areas of your body?

I recommend that you stand naked in front of the mirror and do this exercise at least once a week. This activity has many surprising rewards. Not only does it get you back into noticing and loving your own body, but you are massaging and healing your body with touch as well. You are becoming aware of your body changing. From a beauty perspective, you become aware of the hairs that you missed when you shaved in the morning. You can keep track of moles that might start to change and keep an eye out for any lumps in your breasts - all of which are positives and make you more body aware. The more you are aware and appreciate your body, the more you tend to look after it. You will start eating better, drinking more water, and consuming less alcohol, and you will do more exercise.

On my body I have an area that I used to skip, which was always my stomach. This was due to the fact that after the birth of my daughter my stomach didn't bounce back to how I would have like it. Also with the pregnancy I encountered stretch marks over the front of my stomach. When my stomach was touched by a lover, I would recoil slightly and move his hand away from that area. But it wasn't until I discussed this topic with a very wise dear friend that I realised I was being very unforgiving of myself. She very kindly explained that I should be very proud of the stretch marks on my stomach as they represent my daughter's safe passage into this world; that my stomach (uterus) was my daughter's home for 40 weeks whilst I was pregnant. My body nourished, protected and allowed my beautiful daughter to grow happy and healthy, until she was ready to face the world - albeit at 41 weeks .... she was slightly overcooked ☺. So, I don't stop at that area when applying cream anymore. I continue and proudly massage my stomach (with all its stretch marks) as I smile and feel proud of how glorious my body is in producing such a gorgeous human being.

Even from a male perspective, a friend of mine (I will call him Jack for anonymity reasons) has many scars on his body after years of being in the armed forces. Jack had been shot a few times and had suffered many wounds whilst in the service. He was very hesitant about showing his body to anybody and would try to keep his shirt on for as long as he could. I think his hesitation was a combination of having to tell the stories of his injuries (which was too painful to relive) and was also due to the confidential nature of his job. Jack wasn't at liberty to say what happened or more importantly - where and when. When I first met Jack, he would take his shirt off last and turned the lights down so that I wouldn't notice his scars. He was a physically impressive man - 6'5" tall, with a broad and beautifully-sculptured body. He was handsome, strong, in his early 40s, muscular, tanned and unbelievably fit. He was a very introspective sort of man - exciting, well-travelled (obviously with his job), gentle, kind, considerate, intelligent, dangerous and funny. But Jack was a very tortured and damaged soul and suffered from alarming night terrors. I know it sounds weird, but I always felt that I was never alone in the room with him - that the souls of all the people he had come into contact with during his service were hanging around in spirit; and as if his own personal karma crew was weighing him down and tormenting his mind, body and spirit.

Jack never liked to look at himself in the mirror. He hated his reflection and was the only man I met who would shave the whiskers of his beard with a t-shirt on. Jack travelled a lot for work and would be away overseas for many months (in some instances 12 months) at a time.

But when we caught up it was always intense and passionate. We would always start with a mutually reciprocated massage. Slowly massaging parts of his body with a beautiful blend of lemongrass and almond oil, I paid particular attention to his wounds and scars. I would kiss them first and then gently massage them and then move onto other parts of his body. Over time Jack's confidence grew, as did the trust between us, and he stopped flinching when I touched his scars. Like my stretch marks, his scars were a part of his life journey. They were a part of him, but they did not define who he was a person. As time passed, I'm pleased to report that this glorious and amazing man became confident in his own skin and in his scars. He would jump out the shower in his full glory and look at himself in the mirror as he slowly dried himself with a towel. He looked long and hard at his scars and applied moisturiser to his whole body - loving and accepting every part of his body ..... even shaving naked. He had found his inner God.

Nutrition is essential - you need to eat well and treat your body like a temple. Fill it with goodness, organic foods, cold pressed juices, plenty of water, and reduce the amount of stimulants like coffee and alcohol. Remove sugar and fizzy drinks from your diet. Visit a naturopath or dietician and get some direction on what foods you should be eating and which ones to avoid. Recently I did a food sensitivity test to see which foods I had an intolerance to. This involved having four vials of blood taken and sent off to ALCAT to test and identify my reactions (severe, moderate, mild and no tolerance) to food, herbs, additives, moulds, environmental chemicals and pharmacoactive agents. The results were rather comprehensive - I had a severe intolerance to olives, scallops, snapper and dairy. Luckily for me, I only had a mild intolerance to mint and limes (which when combined with Grey Goose Vodka and soda water makes up my favourite drink). Even if I was allergic, I would be happy to suffer the consequences .... a girl has to live! I would recommend doing the test (it is rather costly) but beneficial. If you are armed with a good diet, an exercise plan and drink plenty of water, then you are well on your way to bringing your inner god/goddess out.

Colour

Add some colour to your clothes, makeup, hair, environment (ie paint a wall) or add some colourful accessories to your home. The use of colour brings a lot of joy to your environment and yourself. Try to limit the amount of black clothing you have in your wardrobe. The significance of colour is below:

- White - symbolizes innocence and purity. It's great for the home environment as it reflects light.
- Red - passion and love. It stimulates a faster heartbeat and breathing. Red stands out and is very sexual and sensual. The use of red lipstick and nails is said to represent confidence, classic beauty and fearlessness.
- Blue - peaceful, tranquil, calming and soothing. It represents the sky and ocean. Blue is said to lower blood pressure, and gives a sense of security. A blue scarf worn around the neck is said to assist in speaking your truth as it opens the throat chakra.
- Green - is easy on the eye, and is calming and relaxing. It represents wealth and fertility. It can soothe pain and make you feel happy. It's clean and fresh.
- Yellow - is bright, cheerful and optimistic and adds a ray of sunshine.
- Purple - passion, mystery, wealth and sophistication. It is also feminine and romantic.
- Orange - is friendly, relaxing and ambitious.
- Pink - feminine, sensitive and youthful.

Be Happy

Have you ever noticed that when you are happy and feel joy that you rarely feel fear, guilt or shame? The happiness that you feel is true and real. Think to yourself why would you want to feel anything else but happiness? I realise that there are people in this world who thrive on being unhappy in a mundane, dreary existence. They normally have a victim mentality and feel safe in the knowledge that if they are unhappy then they don't have to ever be disappointed. They don't try. They are living in a constant state of fear. To me this is not living. It is merely existing and is a tragic and sad way to carry out your life.

Make a conscious effort to be happy. This starts with a simple smile. Never underestimate the power of a smile. It can change the tone of your voice, light up your face and defuse most situations. Identify what makes you happy. Is it the simple pleasures of a well-cooked meal, a perfectly mixed cocktail, swimming in the ocean, going for run, watching the sunrise and/or sunset, feeling the sun on your face at the beach, or smelling a fragrant flower? Maybe it's taking your kids to the park to play and listen to them laughing, playing sport, engaging with family and friends. Or my personal favourite - spending the whole weekend in bed with your significant other, only venturing out of the bed to get more food and drink supplies.

I recently watched a documentary about big wave surfing called *Riding Giants* (2004) by Stacy Peralta as I do have a weakness for surfers. I realise this film has been out for a while now, but it was an afternoon movie during the week and I love the ocean so I sat down, relaxed and watched it. The movie was uplifting because the guys that they interviewed felt pure happiness and joy when surfing, like being in a meditated state. Their eyes became alive when discussing the ocean and surfing. Without any surf they were simply miserable, longing for the next great wave. But what stood out for me was when the world-renowned surfer, Laird Hamilton, was interviewed after he had caught and rode this amazing big wave East of Hookipa, at the infamous surf spot called Peahi or 'Jaws'. He said, "I don't want to not live because of my fear of what could happen". This statement rings true - he chooses happiness and joy over fear any day.

Just Say No

I'm a pretty easy going type of person, and I like to help as many people as possible. I'm not a people pleaser by any stretch of the imagination. You know one of those annoying people who say 'yes' all the time to please and pacify others, forsaking their own happiness. I will help and accommodate friends and family if I have the time, inclination and desire to do so.

What I have discovered is that the older I get, the greater the tendency I have to simply say 'no'. I am putting the needs of myself first and when asked to assist, I question myself, *Do I have the energy to accommodate this person?*. If my energy levels are low, then I just say 'no'. If I do have the energy, then I will say 'yes'. It's not a selfish act by saying 'no' - quite the contrary, in fact. It is making a conscious decision that you are worthy as a person to put your wellbeing first and then give to others once you are able.

Honour Your Own Rhythm

Finding and honouring your own individual rhythm is easier to achieve than you would think. The basic principles to achieving this goal are to honour your mind, body and soul. This starts with identifying what you need as a human being and then operating in a loving and caring way towards yourself. Basically, what works best for you.

Don't be influenced by what society says is the 'norm'. I mean what and who is normal anyway? And more importantly, why the hell would you want to be that? You are a unique and amazing individual who is constantly evolving as a human being. Don't be pigeon-holed into this thinking that you have to act a certain way, dress a certain way and work 9 to 5 (more like 7am to 7pm these days). How many people out there are traditionally-married, have two kids, a mortgage, a couple of cars and a dog with a white picket fence at 40? Who the hell made these rules up anyway?

Again, think for yourself. Sit down and contemplate how you want to operate as an individual going forward. Let's imagine that there are no rules to adhere to, no boundaries or self-imposed limitations. What would you do?

I'll tell you what you would do - you would be fucking happy, that's what. You'd be euphoric and jumping for joy. So, what are you waiting for? Why not start now? All you need to decide is what approach you wish to take to honour your rhythm - either a phased implementation or a 'big bang' approach.

As you are pondering how you wish to operate as an individual, conduct a self-realisation exercise of your positive attributes. Write down the positives about yourself. Most people have difficulty writing down and acknowledging what's good about themselves and tend to focus on the lack or negatives.

So to help you get started, I suggest you begin by searching on the internet for the term 'values'. Don't be surprised when you discover there are hundreds of 'values' - I certainly didn't know there were so many.

Work your way through the list, and read each one to see how they resonate with you? If a particular value does sit well with you, then add that value to your list. These values could include joy, compassion, honesty, love, truth, etc.

Then take a look around and see what you like about your friends and family members, what positives they have that you identify with. Again, if these resonate, add them to your list. Do you take time to listen to others, nurture and to connect? If so, add these to the list.

You're reading this book, so add intelligent, gutsy, and able to embrace change to your list.

Once you have finished compiling the list, read through each one and congratulate yourself on having so many positive attributes. You are worth knowing. You're travelling pretty good so far, my friend.

Now that you have already identified your values (and positives), are you willing to go one step further? Be brave and take the leap. Every corporation around the world has a purpose (normally to make a profit), values, a vision, and goals, and in some rare cases a belief system. All these combined outline how the corporation prefers to operate, what they expect from employees, community and suppliers. The same can be applied to yourself - your inner-self, that is.

Part of finding your rhythm is knowing your inner-self. What is your purpose in life? What were you put on this earth to do? Have you ever felt a longing that you are meant to be doing something, but not sure what that is? Like going to university and/or college and enrolling in Accounting, for example, but in reality, your heart is not really in it. You graduate and start to be successful at your chosen field and have a comfortable existence. But you define yourself by your role as an Accountant, not as a human being. Ask yourself, is that all there is in life? Do you want to make a difference? Do you want to be remembered? Do you want to be doing something that makes you happy, so you don't actually feel like you are working at all?

Following the breakdown of a relationship it is the perfect time to reflect on finding your inner-self and treating your inner-self like a god/goddess. Expand your mind and continuously learn new things, realise what makes you happy and take the plunge and go for it. Get to know yourself as a person and be true to who you are.

I have spoken with countless people on this topic and the majority expressed that they are not happy in their day job - that their job is unfulfilling. And worst still, it goes against their own personal values, morals and vision on how they want to live their life. Colleagues who are cut-throat surround them. They are narcissistic, undermining; play games, are jealous, ego driven and generally suck the goodness out of them. But they sacrifice their own personal happiness and joy for the sake of a healthy income, allowing the mortgage, bills, school fees, car and personal loans to be paid.

Every single person I interviewed regarded having a traditional job as 'That's just how life is. It's what we do, isn't it?' I'm not suggesting you quit your job and follow your dreams ..... not just yet, at least. However, many have gone down this road and said goodbye to corporate life and changed their lifestyle completely. They have recognised what they need compared to what they want. They have embraced what's commonly known as a 'sea change' or 'country change'. They have sold up their 'mortgaged to the hilt' houses in favour of a more downsized house with little or no mortgage. They traded in their fancy European cars for cheaper models and focused on a healthier happy lifestyle.

I suggest a compromise and begin by simplifying your life and finding that happy medium where can you co-exist with your work and inner-self - always keeping in mind your long-term goal.

Your natural rhythm can also be impacted by nature and the energy you feel around others. If I'm feeling out of sorts after spending way too much time in the corporate environment, then I need to ground myself. I do this by going down to the beach and sitting on the sand and grounding my bare feet into the sand. I go for a swim in the ocean which instantly calms and soothes me. My rhythm is no longer unbalanced and can flow again.

Remove the Filter

You have a right to be heard. Voice your opinion and speak your truth. You're not some young inexperienced child with no idea of how the world works. You are an experienced, worldly, life educated, powerful person and have accumulated enough knowledge in your life to voice your opinion. Be confident in your approach. Remove the filter that sits between your brain and your mouth - the one that stops you from communicating your thoughts, longings, dreams, and ultimately what you want.

Choose the right environment and practise speaking out and standing up for yourself.

Be brave and stand up for what you believe in and share your thoughts and ideas with others. An example would be if you love somebody then let them know that you love them. Tell that person how you feel - it is liberating and exhilarating. What have you got to lose? If they love you back then that's fantastic. But if they don't, then at least they know how you feel and that you have spoken your truth and you can move on.

Don't just apply this to your family and friends, but also to your work environment. I realise that there is a time and place for everything, and that if you went into work and told everybody what you actually thought about them, you would probably be without a job and be escorted off the premises. What I'm saying is for you to have enough self-belief and confidence in your abilities to speak out more than you have in the past. Practise each day and see what results you get.

Be Passionate

Be passionate about life! Reignite your spark - and yes, everybody has one. Follow your dreams and do what makes you happy. That could mean writing a book, coaching a kids' sporting team, trying a new career, taking time off work to travel or going on that holiday you've always wanted.

Dreams can alter as you age. Life gets in the way and the practical side of your brain squashes your hopes and dreams and you cannot fathom how they could possibly come into reality. But how will you know if you don't try? If you want to help people or make a difference in life, then stop making excuses and just fucking do it!

Commit to do nothing all day (at least) once every month

After spending years on end filling every waking moment with activity and becoming physically exhausted, I have realised that I just need to commit to a day when I don't do anything at all. Or a 'fuck it' day, as I like to refer to it. When I just sleep in, stay in my PJs all day and fluff about the house. I might have a late breakfast, have another nap, lunch, watch some TV or a movie. I may read a book, do something creative, let my mind wander, get back to nature, read the paper back to front, give myself a facial, have another afternoon nap and decide what I am having for dinner.

By having no plans this allows you to recharge your batteries, ground yourself, relax your body and limit the negative energy that surrounds your day to day existence. Important - turn your mobile (cell) and computer off for the day. Or at least put your mobile on silent and restrict your calls.

Bring out your Inner Child

"The secret of genius is to carry the spirit of childhood into maturity."

- T.H. Huxley

I can hear you ask, "what and who the hell is my inner child?" Basically, your inner child is just that, the child inside you. Think, what does a child like doing? The answer is very simple - to have as much fun as possible.

Remember fun? When you were a child and that's all that occupied your time? (besides sleeping and eating, of course). Having fun is very healing and provides many benefits to your body, mind and spirit. It makes you laugh, exercise, gives you more energy, lifts your mood and allows your creativity to blossom.

Sadly, many of us have forgotten how to play like we did when we were children. But your inner child wants your adult self to have fun, to be nurtured, loved and accepted. It's the mischievous twinkle in the eye that you see in an adult that lets you know that the inner child is at play. You know people who are like this - they are cheeky, joyful, playful, gregarious and fun to be around. So, what are you waiting for?

Here are some suggestions to bring out your inner child to play for an afternoon:

- Go to the park and play on the swings. See how high you can go.
- Have a 'game night' with your friends. At the game night bring out all the kids' games that you played when you were young - you know, the classics, such as Twister, Monopoly, Battleships, Cards, Snakes and Ladders, Mouse Trap, Connect Four, Operation and Guess Who. You will be surprised at how many of your friends didn't get to play these games as a kid either because their parents didn't have the money to buy them or they weren't allowed to play them.
- Skip - I realise you may want to do this in private - or not, if you just don't care.
- Go the zoo or the museum.
- Watch a kids' movie.
- Forgive fast and move on, like kids do.
- Sing out loud - in the car, in your house or in the shower.
- Have a bubble bath - complete with a beer or vodka caprioska, of course. Or add that additional element of childlike wonder and watch TV in the bath, like my daughter does.
- Play with a kid's toy. My 20 year old daughter, Cait, recently purchased 10 different coloured tubs of playdough whilst she was at the shops. She loved playing with it as a child, so she embraced her inner child and opened all the tubs and played

with the dough for hours. It brings out your creativity and fuels your imagination. I love buying Lego for my friends' kids so that I can help put it together. I mean, who doesn't love Lego?

- Insist on having a birthday cake with candles at your birthday each year. My family continues to do this, regardless of age. The kids love it and always ask to help blow out the candles (Note: it's important that you apply the 'no spitting allowed on the cake' rule!).
- Smile and laugh.
- Speak your truth.
- Buy all the lollies or candies that you weren't allowed as a kid. My favourite was the rock candy that exploded in your mouth.
- Buy chewing gum and blow the biggest bubble you can.
- Suck on a lollypop - just because you can.
- Eat ice-cream from a cone.
- Daydream.
- Go on a Ferris wheel, dodgem cars or merry-go-round.
- Ask "why" to as many people as possible. It's worthwhile just watching their faces get distorted as they try to think of a response.
- Play with your kids or your nieces or nephews.
- Eat food out of the jar.
- Play Frisbee, outdoor soccer or baseball.
- Climb a tree.
- Build a tree house for your kids.
- Build sandcastles at the beach.
- Go for a bike ride.
- Eat popcorn and candy floss (I'd stay away from the toffee apples as they are terrible for any dental work).
- Play with a yoyo.
- Watch a comedy.
- Spend the day at a water park and go on the water slides.

Embrace your Femininity or Masculinity

Going the whole arduous journey of a relationship breakdown can be testing for your femininity and masculinity. From my experience I was very happy with my decision to separate and ultimately divorce my then husband. But this came at a cost - my femininity had to temporarily take a back seat. I suppose it's hard to grapple the workings of the femininity/masculine dynamics, but I will try to explain as well as I can.

Physically and on the surface I was still the same, with the more traditional 'branding' of what society stereotypically said how a woman should look. I got my hair and nails done every month. I would always wear makeup and tried to look as polished and put together as possible. I have always worn red lipstick and that will never change. I am happy and relaxed in myself and very feminine to my core. I am never one to shy away from showing my emotions, and thanks to my facial expressions these were always on show (I make a terrible poker player). But due to the overwhelming sense of responsibility of having to be mentally, physically and emotionally strong for my daughter and myself, it impacted the outward display of my femininity.

To begin with, as a child I was never a girly, girl. To my horror my mother always dressed me in the most girly dresses she could find - complete with bows, ribbons and frills. I absolutely hated wearing them ... all except for one navy blue dress that would feel great as I twirled around in it. My parents tell stories of me sitting in my pram dressed in a pink frilly dress on a summer's day, then stripping off all my pink clothes down to my nappy and throwing the said items out of the pram. I hated baby pink, pastels and pretty florals. I gravitated towards bolder colours such as rich reds, gold, sapphire blues and emerald green. I am fair-skinned, so the lighter colours made me look washed out and unwell.

I preferred to play with action men with their eagle eyes, muscled body and short black hair, instead of dolls. I love how things work. I appreciate the engineering components and how everything hangs together. I love cars and preferably classic old cars - to me, they are thing of beauty. I love driving and car racing. I'm organised, assertive, confident, independent, and direct with a high sex drive. I love watching rugby, but I have no idea of the rules (I just like the men and their bodies). Apart from these rather traditional masculine traits, I love being a woman.

I love my curves, my body, my long blonde hair, my smile, my sparkly mischievous eyes and my personality. I love perfume, skin care products, makeup, shopping, spa days, pampering, fresh flowers, silk underwear, beautiful lingerie, flowy dresses, shoes, mid-length pencil skirts with stockings, suspender belts and high heels. I love the features of my personality - compassionate, loving, caring, engaging, loyal, kind, humorous, selfless, loving (unconditionally), sharing, fiery, intense, open, embracing, fierce, dynamic, fearless, honest, sexual, sensual and insightful. I know that all this may sound very stereotypical, but these are the features of my personality and my personal preferences.

But during the relationship breakdown I subconsciously toughened up. By applying the self-preservation shield after the relationship breakdown the gentler, more feminine side of my personality didn't come out to play as much as it should ...... or could for that matter. The masculine side of my personality stepped up, and over, my femininity.

I reacted by becoming slightly harder in my approach by way of a coping mechanism - both in my professional and personal life. I had to fulfill dual roles as mother and father to my daughter. I was the disciplinarian, comforter and nurturer, all at the same time. It was (and remains) a balancing act. Adding another layer of complexity, I had to deal with my ex-husband and the only way to manage those complex negotiations was to be in my masculine energy. So, play fire with fire. I dared not show my vulnerability, as he would sniff it out, and use it against me and attack.

But what I didn't realise and appreciate was that I could still be very feminine, strong and powerful at the same time. Being gentle and soft does not mean weaker. I had gotten caught up in the moment of divorce, and was stuck in my masculine energy. I need to work at balancing both my feminine and masculine energy (balanced yin and yang), show my vulnerability, be my true and authentic self and 'drop into my heart', instead of being in my head. Be the goddess that I am.

For men, it is important to also balance their masculine and feminine energy (yin and yang), be true to themselves, be authentic and connect to their hearts. Be the warrior. Tough ask, but achievable nevertheless. Talking to most of the men I know about balancing their energies, I learned that some men are at a loss as to what ratio of masculinity is needed compared to that of femininity. Is it 50:50 or 90:10? The mere mention of inner femininity to some males is unfathomable, until you start running through the traits, which ring true to them and which they hold dear. Some men stated that they struggle with what is expected of them in this day and age. They are confused. How are they meant to interact with women?

In today's society, women are more financial, independent, educated, well-travelled, self-sufficient - and rightfully so. Apart from the obvious sexual and companionship aspect, men are asking what can they offer women?

My answer to this question is simple - men can offer a lot. More than a lot, actually. They can complement (not compete with) the woman, be the yang to their yin. Offer a partnership, as it were.

As everybody has a masculine and feminine side, every female is feminine featuring inner masculinity. The same goes for males being masculine with inner femininity. The traits of both are (but not limited to):

Masculine

- Place a high value on yourself
- Strength
- Independence
- Freedom
- Assurance
- Autonomy
- Internally controlled
- Self-confidence
- Decisive
- Risk taking
- Needs alone time
- Common sense
- Stronger sex drive and more aggressive sexually
- Rational
- Direct
- Practical
- Assertive
- The ability to look inward

Feminine

- Place a high value on others
- Goodness
- Giving
- Unselfish
- Supportive
- Takes responsibility
- Recognise people's basic human rights
- Enthusiastic
- Persistent
- Tenacity

- Kind
- Compassionate
- Patient
- Responsive to others
- More giving sexually
- Creative
- Intuitive
- Feeling
- Visionary
- Connected
- Closeness
- The ability to look outward

It is important to get the balance of masculine and feminine right. Problems can occur when there is an imbalance. The feminine energy is all about relationship, 'dropping in down into the heart' filled with love, supporting, nurturing and being sensitive to the needs and feelings of others - the goddess. The masculine energy gets the job done in a way that is reliable, trustworthy and protective - the warrior.

My recommendation to you is to read through the list of both the masculine and feminine energies and process them. Personally I flit between both sets of energies on any given day. I can be the warrior and the goddess in one day. There is nothing wrong with that - whatever works for you. I try not to beat myself up anymore with the fact that I can sit comfortably in my masculine energy when the shit hits the fan!

I use the lists as a reminder that I do, in fact, have both sides of the coin covered and that if I express myself freely and openly that I will become a more rounded and grounded individual. If that isn't enough for you to take action, then it's important to note that sexually the best lovers are the ones whose masculine and feminine sides are both strong .... food for thought.

A great deal of research has been done of this subject matter, so please find the time to investigate and research more about what the causes of the masculine and feminine imbalances are and how these can be addressed and overcome. Everybody is uniquely different. It would be boring if everybody was the same, but this is just a reminder not to lose yourself and risk being pigeon-holed into just one type of energy.

Interestingly though, I seek masculinity in a male partner. The more in touch he is with his masculinity (and inner feminine) the more attractive and sexy he is to me. The more masculine he is, the more I operate in my feminine energy (with inner masculinity).

ELEVEN

....

REMARKING YOUR TERRITORY

Your New Digs - One thing that I am very particular and passionate about is the topic of marking your territory. I believe once you leave your partner, having a safe place to call your own and have full control of is of vital importance. You don't want your ex anywhere near the property. You become very defensive and protective of the environment as you feel that you don't want your ex's bad energy to infiltrate your beautiful warm home. I think it's a combination of nesting in the first instance.

As soon as I moved out of the home that we shared together I purchased my own place. Granted, it was smaller and not of the same calibre as my old house, but that didn't matter, as it was Cait's and mine. I made it very comfortable. I painted her room the exact colour she wanted. I furnished the house with new furniture, trying not to bring with me the things that had his negativity ingrained into them. I hung pictures of Cait and my family. I did one picture frame of pictures of her Dad's family to even out the balance, as I thought it was important for her to know that she was part of that family as well - even though I absolutely hated looking at it every time I entered her room. I'm happy to say that picture doesn't bother me anymore. I'm neutral when I see it now. I don't feel anything - no hate, no anger - just nothing.

Places

Memories are everywhere you look - good and bad memories. Places you have visited together as a family in the good times and then places that you visited in the bad times. Different cities, beaches, art galleries, cafés, restaurants, parks, and concert halls. Each individual place awakens feelings of happiness or anger. So I came up with the concept of 're-branding'. The way that I see it is that you replace the old memory of places and things with new memories. For example, when I was at the very end of the marriage, we travelled as a family to Europe. One of the cities that we visited was London. That trip was horrendous. Nothing went right on the holiday - especially in London. It rained, which isn't unusual for London, but this just added to the sombre and morbid atmosphere that engulfed what should have been a happy time.

So, after the break-up the thought of London didn't fill me with happiness. The floodgates of rapture and joy didn't flow through my veins. It evoked a sense of annoyance, wasted money and being on the last torturous holiday with him. I realise that might sound a tad harsh, but that's how I felt. It's fair to say that I didn't enjoy the holiday to Europe, because I knew in my heart that this would be last time we would holiday together as a family unit.

So a few years ago I had a few reasons to visit London. The trip was fantastic. I caught up with dear friends, visited the sites (again) and now have re-branded London from a place of sad memories, to one of fun, laughter and great friends. I've applied this re-branding approach to most places that I visited whilst married, creating new and amazing memories. It is very healing, and if nothing else, when a particular place is mentioned, you will have a smile on your face instead of a frown.

Music

I have discussed this with a lot of people, as every couple has a song. The song that always played for the whole duration of our relationship was very aptly named *Regret* by New Order. So, oddly enough it became our song. I mean, the title of the song itself should have told me the relationship was doomed to fail. But you live and learn. The main words to the song are *"I would like a place to call my own, have a conversation on the telephone, wake up every day that would be a start, I would not complain of my wounded heart, I was upset you see almost all the time"*. So, that song certainly did give me hope for the relationship .... NOT.

I love all types of music, with the exception of Country and Western and Hip Hop. So the music that my partner loved and played always reminded me of him. I found I couldn't listen to the same music for a long time afterwards. One particular favourite was Miles Davis. I loved Miles Davis before I met my ex. But every time I heard the songs, it would remind me of him and it put me off the music. This was until I met someone else who appreciated the brilliance of Miles Davis and the music was re-branded.

I can't explain it really. It was as if the re-branding helped me to enjoy the music all over again. I listened with different ears and enjoyed it. It's the same feeling that you get when you introduce someone to a piece of music that they absolutely love. It's a sense of satisfaction and enjoyment that they appreciate something that you have shown them. It doesn't necessarily have to be with a new partner. You can replay the music by yourself and re-brand the music with new happy memories. The fact that you are single again would be a reason to celebrate in itself.

Furniture and Materialistic Attachments

I strongly recommend throwing out your old marital bed mattress as soon as you can. New love = New bed. I couldn't replace mine quick enough after splitting up with my husband. As if the old miserable karma of the marriage had soaked into the mattress; the memories of me sleeping on the edge of the bed, body rigid and stressed out; getting to bed before or after him. If before, I pretended to be asleep so that he wouldn't come near me. Or afterwards when he had fallen asleep. I wanted a fresh start and a fresh, new bed and I wanted to christen the new bed with a new man. The christening did take some time. But it was worth it.

When we separated we divided the furniture and assets evenly. I opted to have more of the white goods instead of the furniture. So I ended up with the washing machine, dryer, fridge/freezer, dining table and chairs and one bedroom suite. I had the dining chairs re-upholstered as soon as I moved into my new house. I purchased new sofas, coffee tables and side tables and TV.

Friends

Luckily, rebranding friends wasn't that much of an issue for me. I am one of those people who has a good cross section of friends with varied interests and experiences. I find that different people bring out different sides of my personality. The majority of my friends haven't met each other, but are aware of each other, and even ask about each other. I am more of a "one on one" friendship or small groups as I am more private. I prefer not to socialise in a big group environment as I find it very impersonal and it drains my energy.

Because of this I never had to put my friends in the position where they had to choose which friend they wanted to continue the friendship with - either my ex-husband or myself. I know that's probably not the right thing to say, but when you are involved in a relationship breakdown most people feel more comfortable choosing a side. They may still love and adore the other person, but they feel like their loyalty lies with the other partner.

The friends that I made before I met my husband always remained on "camp Gaina". The friends that I met during our relationship remained on my camp as he very rarely interacted with them. So that was easy. He did have a couple of friends that were his from the start. So they remained friends with both parties, for a while at least. I caught up with them after I had split with my husband and I felt a bit uncomfortable when they asked how Cait and I were travelling. They were a wonderful caring couple that absolutely loved and adored Cait. But as we lived in different cities, I let the relationship slide and let the natural progression take effect. Sadly though, I don't think my ex kept in touch with them afterwards either as he never invested much in friendships.

TWELVE

....

LITTLE VICTORIES

No doubt you have seen all the divorce revenge movies where the woman sells her husband's expensive car for $1 and cuts all the suit trousers off from the knee down. I can sympathise with her. I realise that this may sound very immature and revengeful, but I found that by executing little victories when the relationship started to go bad, helped me immensely.

When times are tough and you don't know how you are going to get through the day, remember these little victories during these times - they might bring a smile to your face. I needed to vent my frustrations at the end of the relationship and completed a few activities (not all mine) below.

Victory #1 - Sand in the bed

I was married to an anal retentive Virgo male. Dust, sand and any form of mess were his natural enemies. Order ruled his world. An example being that every night when he came home from work he had this 'need' to vacuum the Persian rug in the lounge-room. He vacuumed this rug within an inch of its life, so much so that the white wool tassels at the end had broken off.

Anyway, I digress, so one of his many pet hates was sand in the bed. In Australia the majority of people walk around their house and garden in bare feet - I do too. So when it was time to going to bed, I would have a shower and then hop in and go to sleep. Apparently this walk from the shower to the kitchen to get a drink of water, straight to our bedroom meant that I had accumulated enough sand to cover the Sydney Harbour Bridge! I don't see how as he vacuumed every day. He would then get into bed, tut-tut and sigh and set about brushing all the sand out of the bed onto the floor before he got in. These 1-2 grains of sand didn't bother me in the slightest, as I was exhausted by the time I was in bed, thanks to working 50 hours per week at my day job, keeping the house clean, running the household, stocking the fridge with expensive imported beer, looking after my beautiful daughter and feeding the dog. So, you see, sand was the least of my problems. But a seed was planted .... he no likey sand in the bed. Tick!

When the relationship was at nearing the end, I needed a little victory to keep me going. One smile a day wasn't too much to ask for, was it? So, I walked down to the beach near my house with a large bucket in tow. I filled it with very fine white sand from the beautiful Marmion beach. I carried it back to the house and stored it under some shoes boxes in my wardrobe. Each night before I went to bed I would lift the sheets up on his side and sprinkle sand from top to bottom. Then I would go to sleep. I would be lying in bed (turned on my side facing away from him, obviously) smiling as he angrily brushed the sand out of the bed.

Him shouting, "I don't believe it. Where does all this fucking sand come from?"

My reply, "What sand?"

This would drive him insane. I never 'fessed up' to this and he never twigged that I was the sand fairy. Little victory #1 complete, tick!

Victory #2 – His Toothbrush

Well, I hate to admit this one, but I have to come clean ... pardon the pun. In periods of frustration my devious mind would conjure up subtle ways to get back at my then husband. Let's just say that he was very clean and very tidy. Some would say particular in fact, compounded by the fact that he was a Virgo male. So, at times throughout the end of the marriage I would grab his toothbrush and brush the dog's teeth with it. Not only that, but I would apply doggy toothpaste (as human variety is harmful to dogs) each time and brush my beautiful whippet, Genevieve's, teeth on numerous occasions. So much so that they absolutely sparkled! Then I would rinse his toothbrush and return it to the bathroom for him to use that evening. Little victory #2 complete, tick!

Victory #3 - Diamonds

This isn't one of mine, but it's an absolute beauty that my friend did as an act of revenge - the diamond scenario. Jessica was engaged to a very wealthy American doctor. He was very handsome and came from a very well to do family in America. After finishing his medical degree he travelled to Australia to enjoy a gap year. This is where he met Jessica. Jess was a very beautiful, tall, raven-haired beauty with a wonderful mischievous spirit and a twinkle in her eye. She was a knockout. David was smitten with Jess and commenced the art of swooning. Jess was hooked and together they had an amazing courtship in Australia and both fell head over heels in love with the other.

David presented as a backpacker and never revealed to Jess that he came from a very wealthy family. Jess was a free spirit and didn't care for money at all. Then David proposed to Jess and she accepted. Life couldn't get any better.

Then David wanted to introduce Jess to his family in the US. They lived in Milwaukee so Jess and David travelled to meet his family.

This visit didn't go well. Even though Jess' inner and outer beauty won them over on some levels, the fact that Jess didn't have a university degree and had come from a good working class family didn't resonate well with David's snobbish family. So they started rolling out the standard "she isn't good enough for you" routine to David. Jess was a bold and magnificent Australian woman and not a 'Stepford' wife. So arguments ensued between Jess and David, which tore their relationship apart. Jess had no desire for money and to prove her point, following an argument with David one day, Jess took off the 5 carat brilliant cut diamond ring and threw it into the river - to make a statement that the engagement was over - that money didn't matter to her.

David was devastated, both by Jess' news and the ring being thrown in the river. Jess had proved her point by not keeping the ring. David then stood up to his family and said that Jess is the woman he loves and he was going to marry her regardless, with or without their blessing. Jess then got a replacement ring that was bigger and better than the previous one. Only a couple of years later did Jess confess a secret. She had replaced her diamond engagement ring with a cubic zirconia, knowing full well that she was planning on throwing it into the river. The diamond was worth US $100k. Jess kept the diamond. So, add 'smart' to the bold and magnificent Aussie woman!

Victory #4 – Sorry Note

A friend of mine played out this victory on his wife whilst at their son's football match. Both he and his wife drove separate cars to the football match as they had finished work at different times. "John" simply wrote a note that said "sorry about the dent that I did to your car. I was in a rush". Then he placed this note on his wife's windshield under the wiper. When the wife returned to her car after the match, she spent about 20 minutes walking around the car and checking to see where the dent was. John was pretty happy with himself over this little of victory. John is still married and has yet to admit it was him. But when his wife annoys him, he remembers this little victory and it makes him smile.

Victory #5 – Eggs

Another instance of childish, but fun, behaviour is the old gluing of the eggs to the egg carton trick. My friend is a teacher and her husband is a very talented cook, and thinks that he should be on a TV cooking show. One of things that he prides himself on making is a soufflé. One day Karen had had enough of Eric's behaviour, so she super-glued all 12 eggs to the egg carton, then sat at the table and watched as Eric started to make the soufflé. He tried the first egg and it wouldn't budge out of the carton, then again and again. Each time the eggshell would break and spill over the place. Eric was furious and ended up throwing the carton across the room.

Karen and Eric divorced two years later.

THIRTEEN

....

IMPACTS TO YOUR HEALTH

Again I'm by not an expert by any stretch of the imagination on health. From what I have learned from personal experience over the last 11 years since my separation and divorce is that a lot of people face a lot of trauma when it comes to relationships. This trauma does not make for a healthy mind, spirit or body. It damages you on so many levels.

I once read that in times of significant trauma the cells in your body can 'switch' from healthy to damaged cells. For example if you were exposed to violence or other traumatic events as a child, the trauma of this event could affect your DNA and leave lasting marks or stretches on your DNA called telomeres. These telomeres shorten a little bit every time the cell replicates until it reaches its replication limits. The damage to the cells has been linked to a person suffering from a variety of diseases .... not good.

But after reading the article it did make me think and reflect. Would divorce classify as a significant event? I know it's up there with giving birth, marriage, death, moving house and starting a new job, but would it be enough to impact your cells? Do stressful home environments permanently affect your chromosomes? I'm not a geneticist, but to me it would make sense. Why wouldn't a significant event cause serious damage to your body and health?

I know going through the whole relationship took an enormous toll on my physical wellbeing. All my muscles became as hard as rocks, especially my shoulders and neck. I suffered from migraines, aching joints and battled with a lack of sleep. The prolonged stress on the body impacted me most when I allowed myself to stop. But whilst you are in the relationship downturn mode you keep going, then when you breakup you have to be strong and keep going ..... so again you continue on - fearing that if you stop that you will collapse and get sick.

But I did stop after the divorce. And, yes, I did get sick as I allowed my body to relax, acknowledging and accepting that my body would encounter a steady flow of medical conditions. But that was OK as I allowed my body to do what it needed to do in order to heal itself.

Your body has an amazing way of letting you know what it needs and what it doesn't. Be kind to yourself and embrace the healing. Your body is a magnificent brave vehicle that has carried and supported you throughout your journey. So you owe it to yourself to give it all the time it needs to recuperate, heal and recharge.

I am also a firm believer that you store your emotions in your body, which can impact you both physically and/or mentally. For example, I have had a lot of physical pain with my right knee for the last two years. So the metaphysical theory could be a combination of *I'm inflexible and don't want to move forward into the future. And/or I am tired of waiting for my life partner to stand by my side.*

I'm happy to report that since I have focused on moving forward and am embracing my life's purpose, my knee has been great. However, I'm still keen for my life partner to stand by my side - someday soon I hope.

So your body has a way of warning you about what is going on in your life. A sore shoulder means that you are burdening too much responsibility. Issues with your hands and/or fingers relate to your profession in life; index finger can suggest you have no direction in life; and thumbs refer to not wanting to be told what to do. Maybe it would be worthwhile to re-evaluate your career and embrace a new job that makes you happy.

A lot of books have been written about this very topic. The holistic approach could be dismissed by some in support of 'it's not a metaphysical issue. I hurt my hand at work'. But wouldn't it be worthwhile and beneficial to investigate further before ruling this possibility out? What do you have to lose?

Patterns

I must admit that writing this book has been a very cathartic experience. It has allowed me to release, heal and move on. The opportunity has allowed everything to be out in the open as I have spoken my truth.

As I look around at my divorced friends there happens to be a pattern forming. I realise this may be a generalisation, but it is purely based on experience - one person within the divorced couple had grown and blossomed and gone down a particular path. The other partner has had the option to walk with them on this new path, to grow with them and thereby complement each other, but has unfortunately either halted or gone in the opposite direction, forcing the two parties to forge a separate direction in life. The majority of these individuals ached for their partners to join them on this path. But to no avail. The other person hasn't realised (or in some cases hasn't noticed) why their partner has gone on this path, passing it off as just a phase - regrettably taking their eyes off the ball just for a moment, and in that instance they have lost their partner to growth - both personal and spiritual.

As is the case in most instances one partner takes more and doesn't give. So the tank is empty. No more fuel for the relationship. Unsure of themselves they move on and find someone new who is on the same path (for the time being). One person may take a while to assess and reflect on what steps to take next. They hibernate for a while, go to the movies, read books, and reconnect with family and friends. Re-engage with their support system.

Then after a few years they come out of the cocoon and spread their wings. They become more magnificent than before. Yes, they have battle scars, but they are thriving. They have pulled through and survived the worst possible scenarios that life can throw at them. They are resilient, strong people.

Then there are the individuals after all they have been through who do not take the time or opportunity to learn from the relationship breakdown. They do not take stock and wonder why the relationship failed. At the back of their minds there might be this little voice that is nagging and begging to be heard. Your mind has subconsciously conducted its evaluation and may in fact come to the conclusion that all your relationships have a common denominator. You seem to attract the same type of person, with the same qualities again and again.

So, let's do some investigations, shall we? Sit down in a peaceful environment, get a piece of paper and a pen and take a few deep breaths. Divide the page into three columns.

1. On the left hand column put the heading 'Partner';
2. In the middle column, put 'Duration of Relationship' in the heading; and
3. On the third and far right column write down 'Reason for Breakup'.

Then go through and list as many of your relationships as you can and see if you have any common themes that tie all the relationships together. Are the relationships more than six months in duration? Did you get bored with the person? Was infidelity involved? Did they have traits of any members of your family? An example could be that you encountered a partner with a combination of traits of your parents, both positive and negative traits. It is an interesting exercise to conduct. You will be surprised by the results, I can assure you.

So, what do you do with these results? If you don't want to venture down this path again and encounter the same relationship issues that you had with previous partners, then I suggest that you reach out to get some professional help. You are worth the investment. The assistance doesn't necessarily have to be in person, even though this is preferred by most practitioners. Skype could be an option if you didn't want the hassle or felt uncomfortable attending an office. But I would suggest contacting a professional in either counselling, psychology, NLP or emotional therapy. These professionals will help you identify the issues, triggers and patterns and assist you in accepting them and working through how best to manage them in future. This will not only benefit your emotional, psychological and physical state, but also assist you financially.

In the long run it is cheaper to invest in professional help, than to go into another relationship, repeat the same pattern and end up getting divorced. In economic terms:

Professional Help $ v Divorce $$$$$$$$$$$$$$$$$$$$$$$$$

It's a no-brainer, really, when you think of it. Who wins? You do. By addressing the reasons why you do what you do, will change the pattern and break the cycle of unsuccessful relationships. You are not only demonstrating to yourself, but also to your friends and family, that you are worth it. You deserve joy and happiness. You want to be the best version of yourself. You're fucking fantastic, for fuck's sake.

Please take the leap of faith and give it a shot. What are the alternatives? Continue making the same mistakes again and again? I realise that getting professional help is a tough ask. Going to these sessions may well bring other areas of your life to the surface that you have not dealt with in the past. Issues may come up about your childhood, and like opening Pandora's Box; memories may start to flood. This reaction is normal and your professional practitioner may need to dig a little bit deeper to understand and assist why you behave a certain way.

From personal experience, identifying the issue is half the battle. I now know why I attracted a particular type of man. I knew the triggers and my behaviours if I encountered a guy with similar traits and I just walked away from that individual. The professional engagement that I used was a very experienced 'NLP Guru'. The sessions started face to face, then when my NLP specialist moved back to Texas, USA we continued the sessions via Skype.

Anxiety

It's strange how physical objects like houses, cars or venues can cause massive panic attacks, don't you think? I bought a new house in the same suburb as my parents and a ten minute drive to both my brothers' places. Coincidently, my ex-outlaws live in the same suburb as well, only 500m away to be exact. Interestingly enough, every time I used to drive past their house, I would encounter a slight panic attack and feel my heart race. The memories of the marriage and the divorce came flooding back in an instant. It was a constant reminder of my marriage. I longed for the day that I would be able to drive by the house and for it to have no effect on me at all. After seven years I could happily drive by and look at the house with no feeling at all. It takes time to go through the emotions of anger, disgust, pity and then nothing. Absolute nothingness.

Levels of anxiety can fluctuate and can occur randomly when you least expect. This can happen when you run into your ex, worry about your future, meet your ex's friends or family, attend a court case to discuss the divorce or child custody hearings or see a person on first glance that looks like your ex. As time goes on, like my driving past my ex-outlaws home, the impact is lessoned. Trust me, your anxiety levels and frequency of the occurrences will reduce significantly over time, resulting in your feeling much calmer and the scenarios having little or no impact.

Stress

I have yet to meet anybody who hasn't been the slightest bit stressed by a relationship breakdown, unless you happen to be a cold-hearted nasty piece of work. I think anybody would be lying if they said that they weren't impacted in some way, as a break-up is painful. You encounter the stresses of your world being turned upside down, your daily couple routine changes with additional responsibilities being inherited. You feel the full range of emotions pulsing through your veins for the duration. Any one day can throw happiness, sadness, anger and anxiety at you causing your stress levels to rise substantially. It's OK - this is normal. Everybody goes through these emotions, like the changing seasons. Ride through them as time does heal all wounds.

Try some relaxation techniques to reduce your stress levels.

- Get plenty of rest and sleep as much as you can.

- Get a message that is relaxing - not a sport's massage - preferably with essential oils (for the guys sandalwood works well).
- Try having 1 tablespoon of powdered magnesium in a glass of water per day. This is a natural relaxant for your muscles and is great for muscle repair.
- Try meditation. A minute's practice per day can alter the brain's neural pathways, making you more resilient to stress.
- Take a yoga class. Start with the more gentler Hatha which combines a series of basic movements with breathing or Vinyasa, which is a series of poses that flow smoothly into one another.
- Breathe deeply. Take a five-minute break and focus on your breathing. Sit up straight and breathe through your nose and out through your mouth. Deep breathing slows your heart rate and lowers your blood pressure.
- Go for a walk on the beach or in the mountains - basically, just get back to nature as it instantly calms you.
- Catch up with friends who are fun to be around, make you laugh and listen to you when you talk.
- Listen to music.
- Just smile.

You may want to think about how you react to stress and deal with it in a more manageable way. For instance, the feelings that you feel - are you in control of them or are they in control of you? It's not worth blaming yourself or anybody, in fact. Use this opportunity as a chance to grow as an individual. The mere fact that you are doing an evaluation of the relationship and identifying what went wrong and how you could do things differently, is huge progress.

You are willing to change for the better by continuously learning and evolving as a person, which will benefit not only you, but also your next partner.

....

FOURTEEN

WHERE THERE IS DARKNESS LET THERE BE LIGHT

"The saddest kind of sad is when your tears can't even drop and you feel nothing. It is like the world has just ended. You don't cry, you don't hear, you don't see. You just stay there. For a second, the heart dies"

- Anonymous

Pain - I think it goes without saying that there are two types of pain in this word - pain that hurts you and pain that changes you. It is inevitable that being in a relationship you will experience varying degrees of pain as you have opened your heart to another person. A relationship brings to the table the full smorgasbord of emotions and fears from love, joy, contentment, affection, awe, desire, tenderness, pleasure, rapture and closeness to anger, betrayal, dismay and hurt. It's a rollercoaster of emotions, but when the relationship starts to go bad you feel like you would rather crawl under a rock and just forget everything and everyone because you just can't deal with it anymore.

The pain that I experienced was more around the loss of the idea of the marriage and the loss of the family unit - the pain consumed me. At the time I couldn't see how I would ever get over how I felt. But that was 11 years ago and I'm happy to report that it is not my current state. I now feel happy and joyous, but looking back on that period of my life, it seems like a distant memory. Granted, the scars are still there, but they are fading thanks to the care and repair and finding my inner goddess activities.

Think about the past relationships that you had 20, 10 or even five years ago. Are you still experiencing pain from these? Has the pain you felt with these relationships changed you now for the better? Are you a stronger, attentive, wiser and more present person than before?

Like the bandaid approach, it was me who made the decision to finish the relationship. He would never have made the decision, even if another ten years passed and he was miserable. He wouldn't or couldn't do it. So it was me who bit the bullet and ended it. This took guts and I'm proud of myself for doing it and letting go of somebody who made me so despondent.

A wise friend of mine once said to me "people are just characters on your stage that is your life", meaning that they are in your life for a reason - whether that be for a short time or a lifetime. My ex was a character in the play of my life and looking back now, I think he played a cameo role and was not a main character. But that's OK.

I have an old friend, Joe, who operates in a permanent state of pain and suffering. He has gotten to the point that the pain is close to destroying him. The main themes in Joe's life are abandonment, mistrust and lack of self-love. It all started with Joe's childhood - his father died when he was a boy. His mother remarried an absolute loser and Joe was left to fend for himself. Joe had no option but to leave home at the age of 15 years and moved in with his best friend's family.

At the age of 18 Joe lost his mother to cancer. So, from the age of 18 years his life spiraled out of control. He went from one short term job to another, whilst going from one failed relationship to another, each one ending the same - he cheats on women and they leave. Joe is now 43 years old. He says he doesn't cheat on each girlfriend because he doesn't love them, but rather he cheats because he fears that they will get too close, see the real Joe and then decide that he's not worth the effort. So, cheating is his way of protecting himself from them rejecting him. He 'gets in first', as he puts it and forces the relationship to end. He doesn't think that he deserves love.

Even being a friend to Joe is intense. He is constantly testing how much of a friend I am to him and he tries to push the boundaries of the friendship to see what my breaking point is. I don't engage in this game with him. I just say that I love him as a friend regardless of what he says or does. This infuriates the hell out of him, but deep down he loves that I'm his friend and that I don't put up with his bullshit.

But being in pain is exhausting for him, so I challenged Joe and asked him, 'What would you do if you didn't have the pain? I reckon you'd be a new person - joyful and full of energy."

His response was *How?* How could he achieve such a result after 43 years of anguish, constant disappointments and heartache? I had to admit he had a point. It was a tough ask - but achievable.

Being that I'm not a psychologist, I suggested that he first speak to a professional to get some guidance, but at the same time add the inner god and care and repair activities to the mix. He agreed to do this, but being the logical man that he is, he assigned it a timeframe of three months. This wasn't much time to undo 43 years of damage, but it was a step in the right direction.

The advice that was provided to Joe was given in sporting terms, which appealed to his sporting nature - wise choice, I thought to myself. The psychologist associated the pain with a physical sporting injury that he would sustain on the field. The steps were:

- Have a break from dating the cheerleaders of the team (very good call, I thought), he could 'self-meditate' for the duration.
- Apply the 'care and repair' activities that I recommended (I was liking this guy).
- Nourish his body with good food and have a lot of rest, just as he would before going into a final sporting match.
- Be kind to himself as his body would take time to repair itself.
- Surround himself with good friends who are gentle and compassionate with him.
- Slowly start to socialise with friends and actively try and learn to communicate (in Joe's case - listen).
- Do things that make him happy (apart from the 'quick wins' of having a one night stand with a woman).
- Go on a holiday to somewhere that he has always wanted to go (he went to see the Northern lights and loved it).
- Get back in the game, but ever so slowly. Become friends with the woman first so that she gets to know the real Joe. So, starting to rebuild his feeling muscles.
- Be kind to himself as getting back in the game may make him feel uneasy. Take it slowly. There is no rush - acknowledge the emotions that he feels.
- He also asked an interesting question of Joe - did his parents ever say that they loved him? The answer to this was 'yes - all the time'. His father used to say that he loved him every evening when he kissed him goodnight on the forehead. His mother constantly said she loved him, but because of her actions (remarrying a loser), he had dismissed this sentiment. This reinforced to Joe that he was indeed loved by both parents - a fact that nobody could take away from him. They simply departed this earth earlier than Joe wanted, or needed. But having them say that they loved him is proof in itself that he has been loved and is worthy of receiving love.

- Have regular checkpoints every month to see if his pain had eased at all.
- Stay focused on the game final - note that he may still have a niggling weakness in the emotional muscle, so try not to rush in and think that he was 'fixed'. Recognise that it was a gradual process.
- For Joe to look deeper into his thought processes so that he doesn't repeat the old patterns.
- Let go of the old relationships that he has had with countless women.
- That through great pain can come great change for the better.

Joe took all these suggestions on board and to his credit he executed each and every one. The outcome of which is that Joe is a happier person to be around. He doesn't take people's shit on board - he is more Teflon coated. He doesn't wallow in self-pity about how crap his life has been. He has taken responsibility for his actions and learned that through his pain, he has now chosen a different path - a path of emotional freedom and less fear. He has also admitted that he cried a lot throughout the whole three month period, but he found this a physical release of the grief and pain that had built up over the years and was not ashamed of this. Like the quote says:

"People cry, not because they're weak. It's because they've been strong for too long"

- Anonymous

Shame

The emotion of shame has come up a lot whilst talking to the people I have interviewed. It's a common thread that plays a pivotal role in people's lives. From what I have learned, people can feel shame from:

- Mistakes they have made in the past.
- The way they conduct themselves on a day to day basis.
- Being rejected or abandoned.
- Being blamed or criticised.
- Ashamed of being ashamed.
- Being humiliated or embarrassed.
- Not being able to do things they think they should be doing.
- Being disrespected or ridiculed.
- Not feeling good enough.

Many believe that shame can be linked to having a negative self-image, low self-esteem and emotional wounding from childhood; that over the years these emotions have been locked away, compounded and not addressed, causing these wounding memories to be triggered at any given time in our present or future. Worst still, to numb the shame, we can turn to drugs, alcohol, or destructive and addictive behaviour.

So how can we reduce the amount of shame that we feel?

- Learn to love ourselves.
- Let go of the shame.
- Heal the relationship we have with ourselves.
- Rebuild our self-esteem.
- Reduce and eventually stop the negative thought patterns (ie quieten the little critical voice that we have in our head).
- Talk to a trusted party about your shame.
- Follow the 'care and repair' activities.
- Follow the inner god/goddess activities.
- Create a positive mantra for yourself - like "I'm awesome" or whatever works for you. I mean you are reading this list, so give yourself a break and focus on the good qualities/skills that you have, such as compassion, kindness, caring, intelligence, warmth, good humour, great cook and good in bed (yes, that is a skill, so don't knock it).

Control

I think that this is the one of the biggest themes that I have encountered in my discussions when conducting my interviews. Control is definitely a cause for divorce or relationship break-up. It is a very interesting one as to who gets the power in the relationship? Should it be, in fact, 50/50 or should the balance be uneven?

I started my relationship with the 50/50 split (or so I thought) and at that time he earned more money than me, had more senior positions than me and was eight years older. Then as I time went on I was in the more senior position and I earned a considerable amount of money, nearly triple what he earned. He would always be eight years older, but I was happy with that.

But the balance of control took hold of the relationship. Not by me, but by him. I think the fact that I was bringing home more money each week than him shifted something dramatic in him. The ego came out to play in. It first started with the bravado. He bragged that his tailor made Italian suits and shoes. He boasted about the amazing holidays, great cars and the house that we lived in - the majority of my salary funded all of which, by the way. He was very happy to spend the coin that I earned and I was at that time happy to pay. It didn't matter to me, because I saw the money come into the house as a whole for the benefit of the whole family, not to be used as some great measure of bargaining tool that could be wielded around on demand.

The resentment started to creep in; snide comments were made now and again. Bit by bit I was beginning to notice that his self-esteem was becoming lower, he got angrier, and jealous. And then he started commenting on the things that he thought he could control in his life. He began to criticise things that I did as that made him feel like a bigger man, and gave him power over me as he tried to make me feel small, inadequate and start to question myself. This form of emotional abuse was increasing. I just didn't understand why he couldn't be happy with the additional funds that were coming into the household. He certainly enjoyed spending the money that was in the bank!

But by this time the ugly side of his ego was in full flight. The nitpicking commenced, he started questioning why I squeezed the toothpaste from the middle and not the bottom (who cares?), why I peeled potatoes with a sharp Japanese knife and not use a potato peeler as it wasted too much potato (again, who cares?), why I left all the lights or power switches on (again, who cares?). My theory was that he was reverting to type, to his genetic blueprint - how his parents raised him and how they treated him. It was his comfort zone, I mean it worked for his parents and they were still together then why the hell wouldn't it be good enough for him?

So slowly he would chip away at the very thing that he originally fell in love with - the beautiful, fearless, independent, brazen, intelligent, lively and amazing woman. Hurting me was his only outlet, as if he was in self-destruct mode.

The control that he tried to exert over me was totally based on his fear. He was so focused on what I was doing that he didn't have to focus on himself. He didn't have to look within himself and wonder why the fuck he was doing this to another human being. It was easier for him to act in this way, as he didn't have the courage to delve into the deep recesses of his emotional wounds, because I don't think he would have liked what he would have found. He wasn't brave enough to shine some light there and try to heal himself. He wouldn't or couldn't save his marriage. But where there is darkness, let there be light.

FIFTEEN

....

CARE AND REPAIR

I can't emphasise this enough. Please, if you choose not to follow any of my advice so far, then at least do this one act of kindness to yourself. When going through a separation/divorce or relationship breakdown it is like a death - it's the death of a relationship. I have outlined the five stages of grieving the relationship process previously.

But what is vitally important to remember is that throughout the process you need to dedicate time and effort to 'care and repair' for yourself. By loving yourself enough to do this, you will be repaired and healed, piece by small piece.

Human Touch

I have always taken care of myself. On the physical level, I had always had my nails done and my hair done every month, no matter what money I did or didn't have. I care enough for myself to get regular massages, facials, go the gym and have a personal trainer and a naturopath. I realise I only have one body and I have a lot to achieve in this life so it needs to be taken care of. The outer layer of my body is nurtured and soothed. I continuously try and work on caring and repairing my emotional, spiritual and mental levels. It is a work in progress and will continue to the day I leave this earth.

Receiving human touch is very important to your overall health and wellbeing. My manicurist in Canberra once told me a story about a more elderly customer that she had. This lady's husband had died over 20 years ago, and she had no children (she couldn't). So every week she went for a manicure with my manicurist, as it was the only human touch that she encountered in her week. Nobody else touched her at all.

This broke my heart. I'm lucky enough to receive (and give) hugs to my daughter Cait, (whether she likes it or not), friends and family and the men in my life. But this raises the point that whilst you are in the turmoil of a relationship breakdown your body may ache for the touch of another human being.

One good option is if you haven't been touched by a member of the opposite sex (or same sex) since your relationship break-up, then indulge in a massage. A proper therapeutic massage is needed, not a 'happy ending' one. If this is the physical release you wish to receive, you can get a masseuse of the sex your prefer. For me it was a masculine masseuse and a very handsome one at that with very strong hands. As much as it was wonderful that he was very good looking, it was more that I just needed the touch of a man on my body as it had been some time since I was interested in men after my separation. I found it very healing to have him touch my skin, work out the knots in my muscles, to nourish, soothe and calm my body. I allowed myself to get lost in the moment and it was a very sensual experience. It was an introduction, or should I say more of an awakening, of what I had missed and thoroughly enjoyed - skin to skin contact. My soul soared as he worked every inch of my body with his hands. He didn't say much. Well, to be honest, he didn't have to - his hands and his physical masculine presence was enough in itself.

Feed your Soul and Not your Ego

Your soul and ego are two very different beasts. Your ego is your self-importance and self-esteem and the part of us that tells us we matter, allowing you to focus on yourself and propel you forward in life. It serves itself, seeks recognition, it feels lack and is insatiable. Your soul, on the other hand, yearns for you to connect and serve others, seeks to be authentic, abundant and to love and realise you are just a small grain of sand in life's big desert. The ego and soul work in partnership with each other. The weighting of this partnership should lean towards more soul engagement and be less ego-driven.

How many times have you heard the comment "he/she is driven by ego"? The comment isn't a compliment. It conjures up a mental image of an absolute dickhead, doesn't it? You immediately have no desire to meet or be around this person. Right? Right.

Your ego is the selfish side of you and cares more about what other people think of you, and it comes from your conditioning since childhood. In 'ego land' it's a comfortable existence; it's safe and secure like a worn shoe. The downside of your ego is that it has the tendency to take over your life and stops you from knowing your inner true self. Your inner-self is where your true happiness and joy lives.

So, I did a search on 'ego' and was shocked to see so many results. The amount of quotes and slogans on the subject interestingly enough all have the same theme:

- *"Want to be happier? Feed your soul...not your ego! Be with people and do things that nourish your truest you"* – Karen Salmansohn
- *"If they're holding onto their pride, their ego and their excuses instead of holding on to you.... It's time to let go"* – Unknown
- *"Stop being offended. Let go of the need to win. Let go of the need to be right. Let go of the need to be superior. Let go of the need to have*

more. Let go of identifying yourself by your achievements. Let go of your reputation". – Overcoming Your Ego, FB/Sue Fitzmaurice

So, feed your soul in ways that make you happy. Visit art galleries, go and see a live band play, go for drinks with your friends, surf, go hiking, read a book, volunteer in a soup kitchen at night time, take your dog for a walk to the park. Do the things that you have always wanted to do in life. Push yourself further than you have ever done in your life - take some risks in life. Feel the exhilaration of your soul being nourished and craving more and more. Once you tap into acknowledging your soul and feeding it with wondrous things, you will find that the benefits are ten-fold. You become more complete as a human being. You are calmer, happier, and more positive in what the future holds, and wake up in the morning with a zest for life ..... thinking *what can I do today?* I mean, if you feed your soul and inner child you are on the right path of a fucking blissful existence.

Be Aware of your Emotions and Thoughts

Become aware of your emotions and moods as you go through your day. Be mindful of any negative thoughts that may pop into your mind that corrupt your emotional wellbeing. Try not to feed the negative thoughts as they have a tendency to multiply. Let the negative thoughts go and bring your mind back to more positive and reassuring thoughts. Talk to yourself. I'm not saying that you walk around like a crazy person and start ranting to yourself. But when your mind wanders and ventures to an unhappy place, talk to yourself like you would an old, dear friend. Be kind and encouraging to yourself. Show yourself compassion.

Try not to blow things out of proportion. If you are feeling upset or sad, simply breathe, acknowledge and accept the feelings, then let the feelings go. Write down how you feel, cry it out or talk to a friend or family member.

When I become emotionally overwhelmed with what's going around me I become numb to my surroundings. All my senses get overloaded and I shutdown. I switch into automatic mode and focus on my breathing, taking long deep breaths to calm myself down. I feel like one of the animals that go into hibernation in the winter, where their body slows its metabolism down for survival, only providing energy to the vital organs, such as the heart and brain. I feel as if every cell in my body is firing off electricity resulting in feeling this intense urge to run from my situation. The primitive 'fight or flight' response takes hold of my body, mind and spirit.

It's taken years of practice to not flee and talk myself into staying, not just staying, but calming myself down. Like a coach giving a pep talk to a sporting team, I identify the emotion that I am feeling (and there can be a lot of them coming thick and fact, so you need to be sharp to sift through and identify which is the strongest emotion). Then I work through why I am feeling like this. What was the trigger? Apart from fleeing the scene, what is it that I really need right now? What am I looking for? What am I avoiding?

Be open to Give and Receive

I love giving to others. It makes me happy. It can be in the form of a compliment, assistance, love, a hug, laughter, advice, presents or my time and energy. But what I fail dismally at is the art of receiving - whether that is a compliment, presents or receiving help in any way. What I have come to realise is that as a child I was raised to be independent and very quickly learnt not to rely on others for help. Asking for assistance was frowned upon, so I became a solo operator. As a consequence when a situation arises where somebody tries to give me something, it automatically makes me very uncomfortable and I try to resist.

On researching the issue many reasons for my behaviour pop up. Some might say that it could be issues of trust, control or feeling of unworthiness when faced with receiving. But I have noticed that not being willing to receive is actually a family trait that goes back generations. From what I can gather both sides of my family have always been amazing at giving and helping people in the community, personally and professionally. They have lived through world wars (WWI and WWII), immigrated to different countries and suffered great hardships. Yet, they have always been the ones with the biggest hearts of gold and willing to give you 'the shirt off their backs' to help anybody, without question. Time and time again this has been demonstrated. But who helped them when they needed it? The other family members normally did. Family came first with the old phrase 'blood is thicker than water', but this wasn't acknowledged as receiving - more like it was just a given that family would step up and help as an unwritten rule.

So, I have had to be open to receiving from others, as this is not a natural thing for me, but I am getting better at it and practise it every day. It aids with the flow of positivity in my life. I have also realised that it makes people happy to give to others (like it does with me) and who am I to reject this gift from these wonderful people?

What has helped me are the following words on "The Law of Giving and Receiving from the Deepak Chopra Centre" [http://www.chopra.com/the-law-of-giving-receiving] that I use and may be useful to you.

"1. Wherever I go, and whomever I encounter, I will bring them a gift. The gift may be a compliment, a flower, or a prayer. Today, I will give something to everyone I come into contact with, and so I will begin the

process of circulating joy, wealth and affluence in my life and in the lives of others.

2. Today I will gratefully receive all the gifts that life has to offer me. I will receive the gifts of nature: sunlight and the sound of birds singing, or spring showers or the first snow of winter. I will also be open to receiving from others, whether it be in the form of a material gift, money, a compliment or a prayer.

3. I will make a commitment to keep wealth circulating in my life by giving and receiving life's most precious gifts: the gifts of caring, affection, appreciation and love. Each time I meet someone, I will silently wish them happiness, joy and laughter."

Surround yourself with Greatness

In the corporate or sporting arenas there are coaches to inspire, support, drive, push and motivate you. So here you are, this great individual that may be a bit battered and bruised from your latest venture into coupledom. Why not look around for people who inspire you? These can come in the form of mentors, knowledgeable and experienced friends, books by experts, videos, courses or life coaches. I mean, why not? It can help you help yourself. Even if you download some books or search on the internet and learn as much as you can - whatever works for you. The topics covered can include confidence, self-worth, work/life balance, managing your emotions, creativity, looking after your physical body.

Don't Beat Yourself Up

Give yourself time and space. Everybody has their own speed, so be kind to yourself and don't beat yourself up if you haven't sorted your shit out by now. It's been over 11 years since I got divorced from my ex and it has taken that amount of time to get to a place that I'm happy. My milestones achieved during those years have been instrumental in who I am today. I was happy once I asked my ex to leave the marriage. But going through the motions of realising what and why things didn't work, took a while. I am a completely different person to the one who got married back in 1994. I can confidently say that I am a better version of myself now. I will continue to grow and become a better human being.

So, please take your own sweet time and work with what tools you have. Seek knowledge and life experiences to be a better person. Don't rush or skip steps to get a quick fix as you won't have a solid foundation from which to build.

SIXTEEN

....

MEN

"Gentlemen, don't invest your love, passion, time and energy into just anyone. The woman you want to give it too will feed your soul, not your ego. She's there to keep you focused, not distract you. And she'll bring peace to your life, not drama and chaos"

- Brandon Alexander

I cannot say that I'm an expert in any way, shape or form on the male side of a relationship breakdown. But from talking to many male friends around the topic I have come to the conclusion that they too are heavily impacted and altered by the whole experience. They go through the whole gamut of emotions and suffer immensely. Like all people, some never recover from the experience. From my experience men process their emotions in many different ways. Contrary to a lot of bad press out there, men actually do feel - some are just better at hiding their emotions than others. This can be generally misinterpreted as not caring or not feeling. Some men just haven't been shown how to identify, acknowledge, process and work through the emotions that materialise.

I think it is a generalisation that men move on quickly after a break-up. But my ex is a classic example of this 'moving on quickly' behaviour. I was very surprised that he moved on so quickly after our marriage breakdown. This angered me initially;

I felt that by him doing this demonstrated that the marriage meant nothing. Or that he just couldn't be alone. But he was alone when I first met him, so this rationale didn't make sense to me. Why is this? I posed this question to many of my male friends and I received varied responses, which I have listed below. These are direct quotes and not my words:

- All because we move fast doesn't mean that we aren't deeply hurt by the breakup. I just couldn't tell anybody or talk about it with my mates. So I kept it to myself and found a distraction (aka another woman) to keep me busy. The quick move didn't diminish how I felt with my ex-girlfriend. It just took the edge off the pain.

- Men aren't like woman. I was brought up not to cry or show any form of emotion as it was seen as a weakness. So even though I'm dying inside I just carried on and tried to get through each day, one day at a time.

- I wanted to feel like a man and in control again.

- My ego - I wanted to feel like another woman wanted me.

- Sex ..... it's as simple as that.

- Just because I don't talk about it doesn't mean that I don't feel the heartache. I think about her all the time, all day. I'm just silent with it.

- I moved on quickly because I was in pain, confused, sad and I needed to feel something, anything really to stop the dull ache.

- My mates encouraged me to move on quickly and "get back in the saddle" with another woman. I slept with a lot of women, but none cut it after "my girl". It was a physical release with the other women. But not an emotional attachment. "My girl was the one. I fucked it up. It was my fault".

- Work wasn't going well for me; the company just got taken over by an eastern states outfit and I didn't know if I had a job or not. I was stressed out and I wasn't feeling like a man or a provider. At the time I was going out with the incredible woman (not a girl) who was warm, feminine, intelligent and funny, and the sex was the best I've ever had. But my mind started playing tricks on me and I started to think that I wasn't man enough to be with her, like I didn't deserve her, that she was too good for me. So I sabotaged the relationship and broke it off with her. Then I went out with another girl (not woman) who was well below par to make feel better about myself. That didn't work at all. I'm an idiot; I think about the first woman every moment of every day. The connection between us was unbelievable. She just got me ..... you know? One day I'll get my get myself sorted and will feel worthy enough to be with her. I hope it's not too late by then. Funny thing is, she loved me and thought I was magnificent, and enough. I wish I'd stayed with her the whole time and worked through my shit. She didn't care about money or materialistic things; she just loved me for who I was. I'm an idiot.

I was never one of those women that once they split up with their partner, they hated all men. I love men - always have - always will. I have had amazing male role models in my life and have a wonderful father, brothers, grandfathers, uncles, friends and partners. So I guess I just lost faith in him (my ex), but not all men. The same would apply if I had a friendship with anybody that broke down. I would lose faith in that individual, but not all friends. The men I have spoken with on the topic of relationship breakdowns have been courageous, warm, tender, caring, heartfelt, compassionate, articulate, engaging and heart-breakingly honest. I thank them from the bottom of my heart for sharing their intimate feelings and hope I do you all justice in my writings.

During my research travels I came across this wonderful article titled *"To all the Men in My Life From My Feminine Heart: a Letter of Gratitude"* by Pippa-La Doube published on the "The Good Men Project" and Pippa's own website - www.pippaladoube.com. Pippa has kindly given her permission to include her article here. I couldn't just extract a few lines, as the entire article is amazing.

"Thank you for being the wonderful kind generous creatures that you are.

Thank you for bringing so much to the world.

Thank you for bringing balance, power, soul, and completion.

Thank you for bringing adventure and hilarity.

Thank you for your generous providing hearts.

Thank you for your courageous strength.

Thank you for your tender vulnerabilities.

Thank you for showing yourselves to us.

Thank you for loving us and caring for us with your huge hearts.

Thank you for providing so generously for the world.

Thank you for being MEN.

....

Thank you to my love for knowing my strength and for knowing how capable I am.

And thank you for allowing me to put my sword down and wield one for me at times.

Thank you for protecting us with your heart and your sword.

Thank you for holding the community so strong.

Thank you for holding me when I lose my shit and can't cope.

The Exit Strategy: Plan. Recover. Thrive.

Thank you for allowing me to cry it out.

Thank you for supporting me through it and not judging me.

Thank you for letting me hold you when your heart is wobbling as well; it's an honor.

....

Thank you for seeing my beauty and for ravishing me.

Thank you for beachside immersion.

Thank you for telling me I look beautiful on the bed in the morning before having a yummy connected ocean side breakfast; this brings sparkles to my heart.

Thank you for opening my heart through your presence.

Thank you for opening my body to pleasure through the presence of your heart.

....

Thank you for always holding an essence of the playful, adventurous boy that you are. Thank you for seeing the essence of the girl that I am.

And thank you for playing with me — it is fun.

....

Thank you for fixing things.

Thank you for connecting the power to the caravan and helping us put the tipi up.

Thank you for fixing the car and helping me change the tire.

Thank you for the little details you think of to make our lives easier.

Thank you for thinking of us with your heart so beautifully.

Thank you for your practicality and generous providing of help as every turn.

Thank you for showing up so consistently.

....

Thank you to the men in my family for keeping an eye on the kids while they're running free.

Thank you for holding my sisters so solidly through their journey of childbirth.

Thank you for being courageous in your depth of love and honor for these women in their courage and strength.

Thank you for helping them find the sanctuary of a breath, by holding the little ones, so they can recalibrate to their own center with deepened presence upon return.

Thank you for being such incredible partners in this journey with new life, I look forward to this experience for myself someday.

....

Thank you to my Dad, for raising me with a real life example of what it is to be in the presence of a kind and generous man.

Thank you for sharing your golden heart with the world and with us.

Thank you for being on the sidelines at every hockey match and for believing in me. Thank you for making me a hot toddy when I'm sick.

Thank you for putting the lights on when you know I am coming home.

Thank you for thinking of me.

Thank you for thinking of us.

The Exit Strategy: Plan. Recover. Thrive.

Thank you for the inheritance of your astute intuition and perceptive nature.

Thank you for being such a wonderful Dad.

....

On this day, I would like to dedicate my day to celebrating MEN. Today, and every day, I sit in a place of deep gratitude for the Men in my life and all that they bring! Sisters let us hold this energy strong today and shower our men with this respect, gratitude and appreciation for the Men that they are, for the gifts that they bring, and for how they provide for us and help us to create such wonder together. THANK YOU, Dear Men, for being YOU! With respect, gratitude, appreciation and love XO My Feminine Heart"

....

Fathers

The common theme from every father with whom I have spoken is that they want what's best for the child/children. They want above all things to be involved in the lives of their children, regardless of how small or big this gesture is. The majority of men that I know (except for two who are each a boy in a man's body) are honourable men.

One particular friend hangs on the yearly contact of birthdays and Christmas and recounts every word that his son said to him on those days. His eyes light up and a large smile spreads across his face recounting the conversation and the actions that his son took. And the fact that he received a simple hug from his son. He talks with pride of his son's accomplishments and has hope that he has played some small part in his son's wellbeing and upbringing that has made him the man that he is today.

I have another friend 'Mike' who has put all his personal happiness to the side to be with his children. Mike is a very fit, good looking and intelligent engineer. Mike, legally divorced from his wife for two years, moved out into another house and saw his children every weekend. Both kids are in their early teens, but the 'weekend dad' visits weren't enough for him. He needed to see his children every day. He wanted to wake up with them in the morning and get their breakfast sorted, make their lunches and drop them off at school. Then at the end of the day after he came home from work, he wanted to have dinner with them, help them with their homework and say goodnight to them before bedtime. He had a discussion with his ex-wife and they agreed that he should move back into the marital home, but live in a separate bedroom. His ex-wife was not interested in having a sexual relationship with him, but they had become friends and she saw the benefits for the children of his being with the family as a family unit. So they discussed it with the children who were thrilled with the idea. But the ground rules applied:

1. Neither party would bring a 'date' back to the house for a sleepover, ie no sex with another partner in the house where the kids live.
2. If either party meets a serious partner, then the arrangement is off and new arrangements are made.
3. That they conduct themselves as a family which involves going to each other's in-laws for family gatherings, such as Christmas Day and birthday celebrations.
4. Continuous open communication about how the arrangement is going.
5. Family meetings with both parents and kids every fortnight to discuss progress.
6. If one of the parties meets someone, then they are able to sleep over at that person's house or go on a weekend away, as long as sufficient notice is given and that everybody is aware.

This arrangement is working for Mike, but to the detriment of his love life. He works long hours, sees his kids every day, but has no time to go out and meet anybody new. His sex life is non-existent. His ex-wife goes out on Friday nights with friends and has a 'friend with benefits'. Mike is counting the years until his kids are old enough to leave high school and go to university. He said he will probably move out and get his own place by then as he made a promise to himself to give his kids the best chance possible to get through high school and into university. But it was his choice, to sacrifice his sex life in favour of being dedicated to his kids' education and wellbeing. I did point out to him that his ex-wife seems to have found a balance - the best of both worlds. He agreed, but he said if he happens to meet another woman then he wouldn't say no, but how the hell is he going to have the time to meet her? And he impressed upon me that there aren't many woman out there who would be happy with his current arrangement. He could be right, but I hope that he does meet someone.

Of course, you hear about cases where either party behaves inexcusably. I have friends who have experienced absolutely horrific custody battles with their respective ex-partners - both mothers and fathers. There are custody cases where the father uses and manufactures serious drugs, is violent, has firearms around the property and is neglectful of the child. Not an example of a safe environment. The case has been brought to the family court with evidence from the police and the father states that he is suffering from anxiety and stress and gets off with a fine and is still able to have shared custody of the child. A mother I know had 90/10 custody of her three children. She has a very serious drug habit and works as a part-time 'lady of the night'. But due to her drug-induced state she has neglected her children. They go hungry and miss school and she leaves her eldest child (eight-year-old daughter) to take care of the house and babysit her six-year-old brother and five-year-old sister. The father of the kids has spent over $250,000 in court fees trying to get full custody of the children. The case is ongoing.

Both parents, please take your child's needs and wants into consideration by interacting as civilly as possible with each other. Many fathers want to be involved in their kids' everyday decisions - what schools they go to, what subjects they are to study at school, venues for parties, and concerts they go to. They also want to be involved in the major milestones ..... in particular the more traditional milestones, like teaching the child how to drive, taking them to sports' carnivals, taking them to the movies with the first girlfriend/boyfriend, or taking them for a drink and meeting the new partners. Attending the your child's 18th birthday party or 21st party. Things that the children had done with their fathers when they were young. Fathers want to feel that the child will remember the key events, just as they did.

My advice to you parents out there is to compromise, where possible. A small act of kindness will benefit all parties - from the child and father remembering a major milestone to the mother who sees a smile on the child's face or hears a heartfelt laugh - memories that they can share with their kids in the future. It's like a family heirloom that is handed down from generation to generation. I remember, in particular, my father teaching me how to drive and his reactions, like holding onto the dashboard for dear life - those memories are priceless. The pained look on his face as I turned the corner and hit the brake at the last minute. These embarrassing stories come up often at family gatherings. Cait is able to share her story of how she learnt to drive. But instead of her father teaching her, it was my Dad, Mum and me.

Unfortunately, for both Cait and her Dad, Cait's father wasn't involved in this major life event as he was (and still is) living overseas. So when the topic comes up, Cait now talks about how she got her licence and how Grandad took her driving and that he pulled out all the same tricks of holding onto the dashboard and the side of the seat in fear for his life, just as he did for my brothers and me. But her father is still missing out on so much of her life story and all her adventures; missing seeing her face light up when she bought her first car and going to the school ball (prom); watching her interact with people, the belly laughs, taking her shopping, and having our weekly weekend breakfasts together at our favourite café. He's missing her growing as an adult and jumping fearlessly into the world.

I know I'm the luckiest woman in the world to witness and share all this with Cait. It just breaks my heart that her father isn't here to share this.

SEVENTEEN

....

AWAKENING YOUR MOJO

I t is fair to say that my mojo took an absolute beating during and after the marriage. I have mentioned previously my ex commented that during the end of our marriage that I had lost my mojo. I hadn't lost it - I just didn't want to engage in any physical or intimate relations with him. I couldn't stand being anywhere near him.

I was still a very sexual and sensual being. But nourishing my mojo wasn't a priority at the time. I cannot believe that I am admitting this (as my mojo is fundamental to my current wellbeing), but I actually had other higher priorities going on at the time. Priorities like planning on getting out of the marriage as quickly as possible and starting again as a single woman with my then nine year old daughter. Dealing with these scenarios consumed every ounce of my dwindling energy, and the last thing I was thinking at the end of the marriage was starting another relationship or having sex with another person.

And there was the problem! After all those years of being married I had associated sex with having a relationship. This is not the case - the two are mutually exclusive.

When your relationship breaks down it is very common for the sex with your partner to cease. In many cases you cannot bear the thought of your partner touching you, so any form of sexual intimacy with them is simply not an option. So, you either "self-meditate", shut off your sexual cravings or seek sexual relief elsewhere. It is important to note that no two people's circumstances are the same and that you should not judge others based on your own personal preferences.

I have friends who have married their high school sweetheart and have only ever had sex with that one person. But once they split from their partner, they somehow managed to cram as many sexual partners in as possible and were open in their sexuality by trying a myriad of options. This can be liberating, empowering and a lot of fun. Stepping down from a long-term relationship, they hadn't explored their own bodies, or their sexuality and sensuality, for that matter. So, here are some things to consider.

Get to know your own body

Before you jump head-first into making a decision, I would first start by getting to know and explore your own body and getting to know it again. For the women out there have a good look around your pleasure zone (use a hand mirror) and familiarise yourself with what you have got. This goes for men, too - have a good look down there. I'm sorry to say that with age, hair colour (yes, you will turn grey), skin consistency and elasticity can change dramatically. Gravity is not your friend. Be confident that you know where everything is. I mean, how do you expect someone else to give you pleasure if you can't guide your new partner into the preferred zones that excite you? For the women - you want the little man in the boats head to be rubbed, not capsized! Yes, you know what I mean.

Body maintenance is a big thing now and you are expected to comply. Decide how much hair you want to keep. All? None? Or a little in between? Do your research and ask your friends or beauty therapist what gets done now? You will be surprised by the responses. There are many options available to you - waxing, shaving, creams, go natural, have your hair permanently removed by laser, bleached or be-dazzled (sticking fake jewels to your pleasure zones). It's your choice, but be prepared for feedback from your partner as they will notice.

Women - I think the majority of women keep the 'side-burns' in check and either keep a landing strip or remove all hair completely. Unfortunately, a lot of women's pleasure zones are being compared to the women in the porn industry standard - complete hair removal with anal bleaching. Yes, it's true. But this is their profession (both women and men) and their goods are on show for the world to see. They have the time and money to have everything looking the best it can be. Wouldn't you make the effort?

Men - from experience I have found that most men, as a bare minimum, 'trim the grass pretty close to the earth' plus leave a 2-3cm shaved circumference at the base, which allows your partner to have skin-to-skin contact with you. Also, by trimming everything (and even shaving your sack) reduces the risk of your partner being interrupted mid stroke by having a hair getting in the way ☺. Some men get the 'crack/sack and back' wax, but be warned, the first few times are very painful. Take painkillers beforehand if you can. But I like men to not touch their chests and have them natural. I find it very masculine. That's my personal preference - each to their own.

But the most important thing to consider is cleanliness. Visit a doctor and get some blood work done to test if you have any sexually transmitted diseases (STDs) lurking. It is better to be prepared than not know. A work colleague friend of mine split up with his wife of 30 years last year and he went to the doctors to get a check up and found he'd caught an STD from his wife as she had had an affair. He was completely devastated as she was the only woman with whom he ever slept. Antibiotics were prescribed and he is as good as new now - just a lot wiser from the experience. So, keep everything freshly cleaned and maintained and make your pleasure zones as welcoming as possible. You want your partner to spend as much time down there as possible, don't you? Trust me - it will be worth your while.

Decide what you want

- So, you're single again! You need to decide what you want. All possibilities are available to you. Only you are the gatekeeper of how far you want to go. Do you:
- Just want a quick service?
- Explore a new body that isn't your ex-partner's?
- Explore all the things that your friends talk about that you secretly wanted to try, but was too shy to ask your ex?
- Move into a new relationship?
- Have your ego stroked and confidence built up by being with another person (or two or three people)?
- Have a break for a while until your head is clearer and you know what you want and need. There is no shame in doing this.

Respect yourself and your partner

Show respect to yourself and your partner. It doesn't matter if this encounter is a one- night stand or a longer term relationship. Treat the person how you would like to be treated. We all have feelings. Be kind to yourself. This may well be the first time that you have sex with another person after being with your ex. This may bring up a wave of emotions. You will no doubt feel nervous, excited, scared, anxious or just keen to get it over and done with. Be aware of your emotions. A friend of mine actually cried - yes cried - the first time she had a one-night stand with a man after her divorce. She had worked herself up into such a state prior to meeting this guy that it was just a physical release, combined with seeing a different man's face on top of her for the first time in 23 years. The guy was very gracious about it and kept going, and held her for hours afterwards as she sobbed her heart out. After she pulled herself together, she wanted to go again and again! See? A little kindness can go a long way and the rewards can be great ☺.

Communicate what you want

Communicate what you want as the other person is not a mind reader. How the hell are they going to know what you want if you don't say? I would start with the basics and then see how they respond, then gradually introduce more and more of what you like. It would take a very confident lover to follow through with most people's wish list off the bat. They are out there, but you don't want them running for the hills at the first mention of certain activities. I normally come from a different angle. I prefer to get one out of the way first, before going into any more detail. That way, I am at least satisfied. And, no, this is not selfish - I am just assertive and know what I want.

Be clear and concise and set the expectations about what you want from the other party. Is it a one-night stand? Just having some fun for pleasure purposes? Or are you looking for a relationship? If you don't like your partner or feel uncomfortable in any way, communicate this and remove yourself from the situation as soon as you can.

Be careful

I don't want to dampen the mood, but you really need to be careful. To begin with, if you are starting to date, then I suggest that you get a separate mobile phone with a different number to your everyday phone. I call mine my dating (and ebay) phone.

Do not set a voice mail service on it either. Sadly, there are some absolute nut cases out there. So the last thing that you want is to meet a new person, do the business and have them stalk you afterwards. By having a dating phone you can screen the calls, they can send you text messages and you still keep your privacy. With social media being the way it is now, do not send any private pictures of yourself via the mobile unless you want the picture to be seen by the rest of the world. People are far more computer and mobile savvy now, especially with social media software having facial recognition. So, if you happen to have a 'private' photo taken it can be uploaded onto these sites and faces can be scanned and recognised and before you know it you are being tagged by family and friends. Do you really want this? That's a 'no', I gather.

If you go on a date with a new partner then I would suggest that you tell your friends or family where you are going. In addition to this, tell the person you are dating that you have told your family and friends and given them your date's details - ie name, mobile and address for safety reasons. That way it's all out in the open. Ask a friend to give you a safety text mid-way through the evening so that they know you are OK. Communicate what you are doing with your date. The same should apply when you meet your new partner and whether or not you should take them home. I would err on the side of caution and not take them back to your place, not until you know them better. Go to a hotel in the first instance. I realise that this may be costly, but worth it. If you do decide to go back to their place, again text their address to your friends and let them know where you are. Then again, another mid-point safety text to say that you are OK. Don't forget this as failure to do so could result in your friend rocking up at his place (with the cops in tow) as you are in the throes of passion. Don't laugh - I know a friend who did this and hasn't managed to live this embarrassing story down for years.

I shouldn't really have to say this, should I? But here goes - no party without a party hat! I don't care how caught up in the moment you get. Take responsibility for your actions. Women, carry your own stash of condoms - both regular and large. Yes, they do come in different sizes, colours, textures and flavours. Also for the women out there, an option may be to use birth control which may be a trial and error experience as to what kind you use, based on your individual requirements. You may not have used birth control for some years as your ex-partner may have had 'the snip' and you didn't need to. But a lot of men haven't had the snip, so it's better to be safe than sorry. Again, take responsibility for your own wellbeing.

Beware the "Oxy Hug"

A lot of people out there are oblivious to the wonderful natural hormone that our body creates called oxytocin. Oxytocin is versatile actor and is produced in your hypothalamus and released by your pituitary gland during orgasm and childbirth. It plays a role for both sexes in intimacy and sexual reproduction. From a maternal perspective, it helps with the birth, lactation and maternal bonding at childbirth.

The beauty of this hormone for women in particular is that when they have an orgasm the oxytocin hormone is released which 'assists' in creating a strong emotional tie to the person with whom you are having sex. Some researchers believe that the levels of this particular hormone can remain high for up to six months into the relationship. It is commonly called the 'love hormone' or 'cuddle hormone'. It evokes feelings of contentment, reduces the anxiety you feel and makes you feel calm and secure. It continues to get released when people snuggle or bond socially. For men, it has been found for the hormone to boosts men's attraction to their partner.

The reason why I mention this is if you are going to go out there and have some fun then try and keep your emotions out of the scenario - beware the 'Oxy Hug'. Some women I know have fallen in love with the first guy they had sex with. You are theoretically a 'born again virgin' so your body will be craving sex and intimacy, and your sex hormones would have kicked in. So, do not confuse sex and intimacy with love.

Embrace Your Mojo!!

I realise that the lists of 'don't do this' and 'don't do that' are extensive, but you need to aware and educated so that you have as many facts as I can arm you with so that you make informed decisions.

OK, it's time to have some serious fun and explore the full spectrum of your untapped potential of being a sexual and sensual being. Experiment and fulfill your fantasies. Trust me, you have no idea what is out there in the world. So what you might think as being 'kinky' may be another's person day-to-day norm.

Experiment

Your body is an amazing instrument which will surprise you on so many levels. From experience I have found that confidence and enjoying yourself is the biggest turn on for both males and females. Your body doesn't have to be perfect. I have yet to hear of a person kicking another person out of their bed because their body wasn't a 10/10! What I will say, though, is you might want to consider working on your overall stamina so that you can enjoy yourself for longer. I mean, do you want to enjoy the experience for five minutes or would you rather be able to go five hours? What's your preference?

If it's been a while since your last 'venture' and you may be a bit nervous and shy in your approach. This is completely normal and totally expected, to be honest. So don't over think it. The earth may not move the first time you have sex; you may suffer from performance anxiety, but who cares? That's what having more 'rounds' of sex is all about. You know the term 'if you don't succeed – try and try again'? Well, that applies in this instance.

OK, let's get down to the nitty gritty of experimentation (pardon the pun). But sex is meant to be pleasurable, fun and enjoyable. It's like that quote *"Anyone can be passionate, but it takes real lovers to be silly"* – Rose Franken. So, what is out there?

- Sexual exploration - giving and receiving, games, role playing and incorporating toys and other objects into your daily practice.
- Sexual positions - these are varied and numerous, depending on your fitness levels and physical ability.
- Experimental - this would cover attending swingers' clubs/parties and experimenting in whatever fetishes take your fancy.
- Aphrodisiacs - herbs, super foods and foods that stimulate your libido.
- Ancient practices - Karma Sutra, Taoist, Tantra and Kundalini.

I will cover all of these topics (and more) in my next book and business venture. So, please check my website www.gainaradford.com regularly for updates.

The main message I want to convey is to embrace your mojo. Each and every person is a sexual being, so go with what you are comfortable with to start off with. Then, as your confidence grows try to incorporate more and more into your sexual routine. It is imperative that you check with your partner that they are OK with this approach. As long as it doesn't hurt anybody, you will be fine. Don't believe everything that you see in the movies or listen to what you hear from your friends. I can guarantee they haven't done 20% of what they said they have tried. Awakening your mojo is an exciting thing. Sex is an amazing healing tool; it has great capacity to heal so many emotional, physical, spiritual and mental wounds. Go and have some fun - you deserve it!

EIGHTEEN

....

THE ALTERNATIVE SOLUTION

'm definitely not a religious person. Spiritual - yes, but religious - no. I was raised in a very strict Catholic family, which has caused me no end of torment and pain. I do not believe in the church's teachings or ideals. Catholicism does not work or sit well for me. The only positives that I took from being raised Catholic included how to apply discipline, try to do the right thing, not to judge a book by its cover, don't steal or kill, treat people how you like to be treated and give back to the community. Religion does work for millions around the world - just not me.

Being raised in this suffocating religious environment propelled me into questioning everything about my own values and belief system. I had to decipher what was true for me and what was prefabricated from childhood. I had to wipe the slate clean and start afresh. I had the basics, thanks to my family, but I had to create my own operating system, follow my instincts and find my own rhythm.

When my relationship started to break down it wasn't the church that I reached for. I found solace in the more holistic healing practices. I can honestly say that the holistic healing approach saved me from the dark abyss. I don't know what state I would be in without it. I openly embraced the healing practices available in my city, country and overseas. I was determined to experience all that was on offer and ascertain what worked for me - it was a process of elimination.

I wasn't new to alternative healing practices because at the tender age of eight years I had suffered a nasty fractured skull injury which left me with crippling migraines, blurred vision and sleep problems. Traditional specialists couldn't explain or provide a viable solution to my injury. Refusing to take 'no' for an answer, my parents set about searching other alternatives to help me get better. After extensive research they came across this amazing man named 'Mr Alex'. Mr Alex was a stately Egyptian Acupuncturist and Healer. So, twice a week I would visit him to have acupuncture and healing.

The result was nothing short of a miracle, to be honest. Gone were the headaches and the blurred vision, and I started to sleep all the way through the night without waking up in pain. He achieved what numerous traditional doctors could not. I was sold - this method of healing was what my body responded to - not the traditional ways.

It was a natural progression that I followed this path when my relationship started to go pear-shaped. I felt excited, like an intrepid explorer, with an inner knowing that everything was going to be alright, even though I was completely exhausted and simply 'spent'. I had used all my strength to manage to get through each day. But instinctively I knew that I needed to go on a journey to heal myself on all levels, whilst bringing out my inner goddess.

The healing process can occur on many different levels - physical, mental, spiritual and emotional. I knew it was going to be hard work, and that it would take courage and tenacity to face, dissect and resolve the issues that confronted me. It is the equivalent to getting a massive karmic 'kick up the arse'. You make a lot of progress and then once achieved, another hurdle comes up that you need to address. But you feel an empowering sense of achievement throughout the journey.

Clearing

I began by clearing out as many things as possible that didn't sit well with me. I started with those people who surround me, except for the ones who I knew were 'keepers'. I wrote down a list of my friends, family members and work - the list was fairly extensive. I then wrote some criteria on which to assess each individual and relationship. Like evaluating a vendor for a tender in the corporate world, I placed weightings (out of 100 - a percentage) on each item based on priority - of what was important to me.

Name of Individual			
#	Criteria	Yes/No	Weightings
1	Do they mirror the values that I have?		20
2	Do they make me happy and bring out the best in me?		20
3	Will they support or hinder my future path?		10
4	Do they challenge me to grow and evolve?		10
5	Do they take more from me than they give?		5
6	Do they add to or detract from my life?		5
7	Do they really listen to me or just give me lip service?		5
8	Do they drain all my energy?		5
9	Are they selfish?		5
10	Do they care or just fake being my friend?		5
11	For my work colleagues - would I be friends with them or keep in touch with them outside of work?		5
12	Do I have anything in common with them?		5
		TOTAL	

"I no longer have the energy for meaningless friendships, forced interactions or unnecessary conversations"

- www.funnyplace.org

By running through the people in my inner and outer circle, it became very clear to me who nourished me and who didn't. I couldn't argue with the results in the table. I set about detaching myself from the friends and work colleagues who no longer served my highest good. The term I used was 'culling'.

So, I culled so-called friends and work colleagues. I either sat down with them and ran through why I didn't want to continue the relationship or just stepped back and allowed the relationship to fade naturally. It was such a relief. I didn't fully comprehend how so many of my friends were draining the life force out of me.

In some instances I had some friends for a long time (years, in fact), but we had not grown together (like my marriage) and didn't share the same values anymore. This was nobody's fault - it just happened.

It was sad to see those friendships dissolve, but I wished them well. I kept reminding myself that people come into your life for a reason, whether that be for a short or long duration - that's life.

For work colleagues, I remained professional and friendly, but just distanced myself from them and didn't divulge too much of my personal life and information.

I understand with family members you cannot just exclude them from your life, if you genuinely love and care for them. But what you can do is step back from them and disengage from the day-to-day drama that they create. Consciously monitor how much of yourself you give to the family dynamic and conduct yourself with love and compassion to these beautiful beings.

By following the culling exercise my list of inner and outer circle was more manageable. I am able to offer a higher quality relationship to each and every one of them. I don't get as caught up with the noise as much, but I am there to love, support and care for each of them to the best of my ability.

I began opening myself up to new people entering my life. People who naturally met the criteria, without me even realising it or assessing them. I was attracting goodness - like attracts like, I suppose. I was also more honest in my dealings with people. I spoke my truth, and the filter from my brain to my mouth became more flexible. I found my voice and said what I needed to say to the individual or group, which received mixed results.

I was on a roll. The relationship side of things was becoming lighter and more fulfilling. What I needed then was to turn my attention to the other areas of my life. My home environment was the next cab off the rank, so to speak.

So, I started by 'spring cleaning' (even though it was winter) my house. I went through every room of my house (including the garage) and started to throw out (by way of selling, donating or putting in the rubbish) clothes, shoes, furniture and items that were surplus to requirements. I was subconsciously shedding what I no longer needed in my life. It was incredibly liberating. I was becoming lighter and happier - no longer dragged down or buying into what society said that I needed in my life.

I noticed that I had a strong desire to clear the noise from my life. I stopped reading the daily newspapers, or watching the nightly news and movies that I found depressing and negative. The newspapers and news items seemed to focus on bad events around the world with only the odd good news story thrown in, to lull you into a false sense of security that the world really isn't that bad after all. I understand that we are surrounded by horrendous world events, such as wars, famines, suffering, deaths and natural disasters that break my heart as a human being. But what about inspirational stories that give the human race hope? Stories that are filled with amazing acts of kindness, joy, compassion, of service to the community - genuine heartfelt stories. I suppose it doesn't make for good television.

Treat your Body as a Temple

I was becoming more aware of how my body operated and was naturally being drawn to areas of my life that needed to be improved - nutrition, exercise and healing. So, the next item on my mental checklist was my physical body. The thought came to me what if I could get nutrition, healing and exercise all in one?

I delved further into this notion and found a Personal Trainer (PT) named Adam who was all of the above. He was a qualified naturopath, massage therapist, Reiki Master and NLP practitioner and PT rolled into one. Woohoo! I had hit the jackpot!

I made an appointment with Adam, who was quite literally a one-stop-shop. He was charming, personable, easy going (thanks to being a surfer), qualified and extremely knowledgeable. I briefed him on what I wanted and advised him that the traditional method of 'boot camp shouting' would not work with me - not unless he wanted me to retaliate and shout back at him. He agreed. So Adam conducted a naturopathic assessment of my health and made recommendations on what natural supplements I should use. You see, the years of working long hours, suffering from a few motor vehicle accidents, sporting injuries, and being in an unhealthy relationship had taken its toll on my adrenal glands and muscles. Basically they were fucked. I was running on my nerves and totally exhausted my adrenal reserve tank. In addition to that my muscles were low on magnesium. So, powdered magnesium and adrenal fatigue supplements were recommended.

I started to feel instantly better, even though Adam suggested that the supplements would take months to build up within my body. I mean, I had hammered my adrenals for over 20 years - this wasn't going to be quick fix.

My three visits per week to Adam after work commenced. I was happy in the routine; we developed a great banter and became friends. The benefits included improved fitness, education, nutrition and I received a massage at the end of the session. Adam provided a holistic approach to the mind, body and spirit and was a font of knowledge. Where he lacked expertise in a particular area (such as a woman's hormones), then he would recommend a specialist who could assist me.

Happily, my physical body was starting to be nourished. Adam recommended organic foods and juices and to cut sugar out of my diet. I started shopping at the farmers markets for organic produce, found a brilliant organic cold pressed juicing company in Perth and ordered enough juices from them for the week. I was getting physically fit and supplying myself with the organic produce that would fuel my body.

So, what was next? Physical health - which came in many forms. I discovered a great deep tissue massage therapist named Chris. She was amazing, graceful, warm, and knowledgeable and had incredible hands. Every Thursday evening after work I had an appointment with Chris so that she could massage my tired and weary body, which involved a combination of hot stone and deep tissue massage. Again, the years of stress had managed to knot every single muscle in my body. It was excruciatingly painful to work my rock hard muscles. The worst impacted were the muscles around my breasts, which had become tight and sore from supporting my E cup sized breasts since I was fifteen years old. Week by week my muscles became looser, more flexible, and subtle which greatly improved my muscle mobility.

A friend suggested that it would be worthwhile to have weekly reflexology sessions, which is based on the principle that certain parts of the body reflect the whole. These points respond to pressure, stimulating the body's own natural healing process and unblock the energy flow for better health.

Naturally, I made some investigations and stumbled across a lady named Sam. Sam was a warm, generous and amazing reflexologist, with a gorgeous boxer dog named Stacey. Every Wednesday morning before work I had a reflexology session with Sam. Combined with the massages, PT sessions, naturopathic supplements, magnesium and the PT gym sessions, my body was beginning to soar.

My 'temple' was no longer in ruins; it was slowly being rebuilt, bit-by-bit. It was becoming stronger and more resilient. The foundations were being rebuilt - physically at least.

But what about emotionally, spiritually and mentally? Surely there were other complementary healing practices that could assist in rebuilding my temple? I spoke with a lot of friends and family, but nobody seemed to know anything about alternative practices for healing.

You guessed it - I started to do more research on other therapies and to my delight found and tried the following.

Neuro-linguistic programming (NLP)

NLP relates to how we live our lives, our patterns of behaviour and communication. So being that Adam was an NLP practitioner, I asked him who he would recommend. Ordinarily, I would have asked Adam, but I decided that he had enough on his plate with what I had already asked of him. He recommended his NLP master trainer and practitioner, Gary. Gary is also an international keynote speaker, communication, team performance, corporate consultant and professional coach. Gary is a specialist in this field and is internationally recognised. As coincidences go, Gary (who is normally working out of the USA) was in Perth for a few months. So, I contacted Gary and booked myself in for some sessions to look at any patterns from childhood that needed to be identified, addressed and resolved. Gary was welcoming, wise, astute, highly intelligent and flexible in his approach with me. I'm a complex individual who has over a lifetime managed to compartmentalise all my emotions. So with Gary's unwavering patience, he worked out what made me tick - he just got me. I had a few sessions with him whilst he was in Perth. Then when he moved back to the US on a fortnightly (Skype) basis thereafter for more professional coaching for my books and business ventures.

Homeopathic Meridian Science (HMS)

On conducting research I came across Homeopathic Meridian Science (HMS), which is a combination of kinesiology, acupuncture (without the needles) and homeopathic principles. The man, Dan McNair (Prof. Dr H.M.Sc., PhD (Hom.Ac),VP) who had devised the treatment just happened to be living in Perth at the time. Dan sadly passed away some years ago. But for a couple of years I would venture to his practice where he would strategically place several small round adhesive patches (like bandaids), which activated with homoeopathic remedies on acupuncture points on my arms to shift my body's electrical system back into balance, so that my body could heal itself.

Colonic Irrigation

Where to start on this little beauty of a topic? Undergoing this treatment was a recommendation by Adam, my PT. The purpose of colonic irrigation is to cleanse the toxins built up in your body due to the fact that we have diets that are low in fibre and high in processed foods, fatty meats, refined sugars and toxic chemicals. I decided 'nothing ventured, nothing gained' - I'll give it a go! So, off to a recommended establishment in Perth I went and I was pleasantly surprised to find that it was professionally run - thank fuck for that! I mean, they deal with waste from people's bodies. So with this in mind, they managed to make a very unsavoury topic the best experience possible.

So that you don't freak out and are better prepared, I will run through the scenario. Basically you go into a private room, remove your clothes (women keep their bras on) and put on the clean t-shirt that is provided. You then lay down on this specially made bed that is half bed and half toilet (?) and put each one of your legs around the toilet end. Then you place the irrigation tube up your arse (that has been pre-lubricated with Vaseline) and then pull a sheet over your lower half of your body for privacy. They provided me with a heat pack and an electrical massage appliance to place over my stomach to 'get things moving', if needed. Then water gets gently pumped into the irrigation tube and outflows your waste. For those who are game enough you can watch the tube with all your waste flowing through, if you so desire. This was just too much for me, so I turned away and tried to relax as best as I could.

I had one colonic irrigation per week for three weeks. I was skeptical at the beginning to see if this was going to be of benefit to me, but immediately after the first session I felt energised and, oddly enough, 'internally clean'. The receptionist did make an interesting point that particular foods don't digest and can 'sit' in little pockets in your system rotting. That comment alone was incentive enough!

For some reason at a work function dinner party, the group got onto the topic of colonic irrigation (for the life of me I can't remember what conversation thread got us there) and I was surprised that I wasn't the only one who had gone down this path. Out of eight people at the table, five had taken the plunge! Granted, it isn't a topic that most people talk about over the dinner table (or anywhere else for that matter) and understandably so - but I highly recommend it. Whether you tell anybody about it or not, is your business.

Emotional Freedom Technique (Tapping)

I was also curious about how 'tapping' or EFT works. I had heard a lot about this healing practice and so, once again, I did some research and found a local practitioner in Perth named Beth. EFT is the psychological acupressure technique based on the same energy meridians used in traditional acupuncture (but without the needles). It is used to optimise your emotional health, remove negative emotions and implement positive goals. This is done by tapping with your fingertips parts of your body, namely the head and chest, whilst saying positive affirmations. Well, acupuncture worked for me with Mr Alex and it seemed something that I could practise on myself. There were also many videos on the Internet that supported the theory. So, what the hell? I had a couple of sessions with Beth in person and then later using Skype, and I came away with an overall sense of calm, and at the same time feeling more awake and alive.

Reiki

The healing practice, Reiki, has fascinated me for the past 15 years. The concept of having 'healing hands' seemed logical and natural to me. Reiki is a form of 'hands on healing' that channels the universal life energy and heals the mind, body and spirit and assists the body's own ability to heal itself physically. I have had many Reiki sessions over the years and found the sessions to be extremely relaxing and calming, and it is the only practice that has managed to calm my mind.

I took my love of Reiki to the next step and enrolled into a Reiki Level 1 course with a couple of girlfriends recently. A very well-respected and experienced Reiki Master Trainer gentleman ran the course here in Perth. The two-day course was amazing. The other class participants were a wonderful group of people who were all beautiful and compassionate people. I couldn't contain my joy when I felt the warm flow of energy through my body and out through the palms of my hands, combined with a tingling sensation in my fingers. The other recipient of the treatment felt the warmth through my hands and felt deeply relaxed and experienced a feeling of wellbeing.

By the end of the course everybody was qualified to practise Reiki. Since then I have been practising on my daughter, friends and the animals. The erratic and flighty cats are calm, and purr during the session. I have been practising on myself each morning and evening and I have found that at night I have been having the deepest and uninterrupted sleeps I have ever experienced. In the morning the session prepares my body and mind for the day in a calming approach before I go out into the chaos of everyday life. If you simply want the benefits of self-healing and to sleep well, I would recommend enrolling yourself in a Reiki course. I have since been initiated into the Second Degree of the Usui System of Reiki Healing and am a qualified practitioner. I hope in a couple of years to become a Reiki trainer.

The other healing practices that I have tried have been various types of yoga, pranic healing, acupressure, acupuncture, aromatherapy, sound therapy, crystal therapy, clearing of chakras, various massage techniques, Chinese medicine and Bach flower essences. I think for me if you receive one source of healing you are then open to other forms of healing. My advice is to try the ones that resonate with you. Give them a go. Some will work for you, like Reiki, NLP, tapping, acupuncture, crystal, chakra clearing, massage and yoga did for me, whereas pranic healing and

Chinese medicine did not. It comes down to whatever you are comfortable with, and noticing that you feel better afterwards.

The alternative approach helped me balance my physical, emotional, mental and spiritual self, which has resulted in a more balanced and better version of myself.

NINETEEN

....

PURPOSE IN LIFE

*"Your life has purpose. Your story is important. Your dreams count.
Your voice matters. You were born to make an impact."*

- theloveyourselfchallenge.tumblr.com

Going through all the physical, emotional, spiritual and mental healing and growth awakened the creative side of my brain that has been dormant for some time. In addition to questioning everything from how I was raised, to what values I operated by, it dawned on me - what was my life's purpose? What was I put on this earth to do? It wasn't just to be the best version of myself, be a wonderful mother, daughter, sister, friend and lover - it was more than that. By following my healing journey I had surrounded myself with people who are following their dreams and being their true self. They had found their life's purpose - it was starting to rub off on me.

So, I thought to myself - what can I contribute? What am I good at? The logical side of my brain immediately reverted back to my profession as a Program Manager/Senior Project Manager. That was my profession, specialising in delivering projects that provide business benefit. But it was not my passion.

The idea that popped into my head was how much I enjoyed helping others. Friends would come to me seeking counsel on a variety of topics such as divorce, holistic healing, sexuality, sensuality, sexual healing and relationships. So, what could I do with this skillset to educate and heal as many people as possible?

Well, a book incorporating these themes would be the logical first step - hence this book on divorce. But I needed to take this a step further. So, I have a series of novels that I am working on and a business venture that incorporates relationships with sexuality, education, love, rapture, wisdom and freedom.

Life has a way of setting you on the right path at a time that isn't convenient for you. You see, I thought I had it all going on. I was merrily working through my books, business strategy and ideas, but hadn't progressed much further - I wasn't focused on my purpose. I had become stagnant in the delivery timeframe for my personal business venture. I was working full time as Program Manager, whilst slowly renovating my home that I shared with my daughter and working on my own personal healing journey. Life was going perfectly. I had a great house, job, friends, family, the car I always wanted and a string of lovers. But my everyday life had overtaken my life's purpose. So the universe decided to kick my arse (without consulting me), forcing me back on track.

In May 2015 three men broke into my home. One assailant came into my bedroom whilst I was sleeping, woke me up and stole the car keys to my daughter's car, as well as cash and both our mobiles. They then quickly took off with Cait's car.

My daughter's car was found the next day - with $6000 worth of damage. Luckily, my daughter and I were not physically harmed during the break in, and nor were the pets. But this set about a chain of events.

The house - neither my daughter or myself felt safe in our home anymore. It has spurred us on to renovate quickly, sell and move on. A large two-storey five-bedroom, four-bathroom home with a games room and pool is excessive for two people. The home has served us well for the past five years, but it is now time to find greener pastures, but still with ocean views as I need to be near the ocean, otherwise I don't sleep well.

Authority - I'm not sure if you have experienced this. But whenever my daughter or I came across any police officers I would automatically think I had done something wrong. I would become slightly nervous. But after the break-in, this feeling completely disappeared. Both of us now have no respect for authority whatsoever. I understand that some individual police officers 'tried' to do whatever they could. But as the Senior Detective stated, "your case just isn't a priority". So, a complete home invasion and the theft of a vehicle, which has left both my daughter and myself angry and emotional scarred, isn't a priority? Nice. That's where my taxes go.

Then, in September my health started to be impacted. I went to my gynecologist and had a pap smear test which was clear, but there were still problems, so I was referred to have more scans with the use of internal camera (yes, up it went!) where they discovered that I had numerous ovarian fibroids. One, in particular, was very large and growing at an alarming rate. They all had to be surgically removed as quickly as possible. Luckily enough, after an agonizing wait, the biopsies of the fibroids found them to be non-cancerous. Phew!

Anger - I was overcome with waves of anger at the injustice of the break in and the audacity of the culprits. The police had made little progress with only a couple of arrests. The court system was a joke and the assailants received little or no sentencing.

It soon became apparent that all these events had snowballed into one big shit storm. Then a very wise friend of mine commented that I was looking at these life-changing experiences all wrong. I was coming from a position of lack and not a position of gratitude. All the nasty experiences were forcing me onto my rightful path in life. Because I hadn't acted quickly enough, the universe stepped in and took control.

The points that she raised were valid:

- Neither Cait nor I were hurt in the incident.
- I was looking at selling the house anyway, as Cait was planning on travelling overseas next year - so a large home wasn't needed anymore.
- The items stolen were only material items and could be replaced.
- I had growled and shouted at the assailant that came into my bedroom and pretty much scared him shitless. He didn't take my power from me.
- The police are only human - under-resourced and under-paid.
- My health was great. I didn't have cancer.
- Both Cait and I are strong women who can face and conquer anything.
- The events have brought to light amazingly unwavering bouts on kindness, support, compassion, generosity of spirit from those people who have rallied around us.
- The removal of materialistic items (car and home) from my life is very freeing. I have nothing tying me down - no responsibilities - so I am free to do whatever and whenever I want.
- Proof that both Cait and I are loved.
- These events have set a strong foundation for anything life throws at either of us in the future.

I have friends who faced life-threatening diseases and circumstances which have made them stop and think - what is life all about? This has put the wheels in motion to reprioritise what is important in their lives. Family is normally what comes first, then health and happiness and joy. The work/life balance is adjusted with materialistic items such as the best car, home and boat being downscaled or sold. But do you need to go through all these unfortunate events for you to find real happiness and realise your purpose in life? So, what about finding a happy medium?

Identify what you enjoy doing? What you are you passionate about? What do you love? It may be one or many things. It doesn't mean that you quit your current job and go head first into this venture, but if you are financial enough to do this, then great. Most of us are not that lucky. You might enjoy being a volunteer for a charity helping others. A friend of mine identified her life's purpose as being the best possible mum to her four children. She grew up in a foster home, so to her raising four magnificent little humans to be even greater adults is her purpose.

You may ask yourself what talents, desires or qualities do I have to contribute? The answer is you have many. Are you good at communicating, organising, listening, teaching, coaching or caring? All these qualities can be put to good use. Just start - get off your arse and take action. Be brave - ignore all the 'what ifs', and try not to over-think it. It's not meant to be that hard. If it helps, (and this may sound morbid) what would you like to be remembered for? What is your legacy?

I recall an exercise that I learnt at one of those corporate team-building courses. You know the ones - where you have to build a bridge over a river with a piece of string, one piece of wood and a bucket? Yes, I absolutely hated doing them .... but anyway. The only thing that I remember is that the facilitator asked each of us to write on a blank piece of paper "What is my true purpose in life?" Next, we had to write the first thing that popped into our heads - whatever sprang to mind. Then, if we didn't like the answer, we had to keep writing other responses until we found an answer that made us cry. The response that brought me to tears was my purpose. I remember at the time thinking that there is no way in hell I am going to cry in front of a group of senior management. But when I wrote "to help others", down came the tears. I didn't know how I was going to help others, but that was what I wrote. My colleague next to me wrote a flurry of responses - over two pages worth. He didn't find a response that made him cry. But he did take home his notes at the end of the day. I often wonder if he ever did identify his purpose in life and if he followed this through?

When you start going down the path of your life's purpose you automatically start to feel happier. When you follow your purpose, you will find that you have more energy and clarity, and you will be inspired and more motivated than you have been in a long while.

It's deeply satisfying to come full circle in a relationship. To have weathered the storm and come through stronger and more magnificent than before. Better still, it is a chance to demonstrate how far you have come in front of your ex and better still, your daughter.

I had such an opportunity at Cait's 18th birthday lunch. I asked Cait a few months beforehand what she wanted to do for her 18th, as in Australia it is a major milestone. In addition to be being the legal age to drink and vote, it is a rite of passage - signs that Cait was becoming an adult. I asked what would she like to do to celebrate her birthday. She responded by saying that she wanted to have lunch with both her parents. I must admit my first thought was "fuck, fuckity fuck", as I hadn't seen her Dad for a long time. But this wasn't about me or her Dad, for that matter. It was a celebration of Cait reaching her 18th birthday and she wanted to have her first 'official' drink in a nice restaurant with French champagne. So, I contacted her Dad who was living interstate at the time and relayed Cait's wishes. He agreed and flew over especially for the occasion.

On the day of her birthday Cait looked drop dead gorgeous (as always), but this particular day she just glowed with happiness. She wore a beautiful dress, high heels, and her makeup and hair were done to perfection. So, Cait and I drove to the restaurant, as we had arranged to meet her Dad there. The restaurant was very busy and we made our way to the bar where her Dad was sitting. The look on his face when he saw Cait was just wonderful - he was beaming with pride at the beautiful young woman she had become. Her Dad asked what she would like to drink and she asked for a cocktail. The barman then asked her for identification to prove that she was, in fact, 18 years old. She proudly retrieved her driver's licence from her handbag and showed the barman, who congratulated Cait on turning 18! The waitress showed the three of us to our table and we had the amazing lunch together. The food was delicious and Cait tried another cocktail then the French champagne was brought out to celebrate. Cait was so happy to witness both her parents interacting and putting all our differences aside for her happiness. It was just one of those moments in life that I will always remember, as will her Dad - a milestone moment that Cait could recall for the rest of her life that included both her parents.

Yes, I have come full circle in the relationship stakes. I entered and exited the relationship with the same vigour and enthusiasm in equal measure. It has been one hell of a ride, and I am a better person for it. I wouldn't change a thing. I am proud to say that I am the best mother, daughter, sister, friend, colleague and lover that I can be. I will always strive to learn, heal and grow as a human being.

I hope you have found this very personal account of my relationship to be of help to you. If it was not for you, then maybe you are meant to recommend it to another.

Thank you for taking the time to read it and I trust you strive to be best version of yourself that you can be. Tick, tick, done....done.

ACKNOWLEDGEMENTS

I would like to thank the following people who have helped me enormously over the years to get to the point of publishing this book. Without their unwavering support, good advice, practical suggestions and differing perspectives, I would not have been able to pull this together. So, to each and every one of you - thank you.

These include (in no particular order) the following - Adam, Liz, Gary, Arturo, Paul BB, Joe, Mike and Jack. To all the many interviewees who so kindly shared their stories for inclusion into the book. To my Rive Gauche ladies - Jo, Anne and Liz. Also, Miriana, Janey, Paula, Steve P, Phil B, Sheryle, Sam, Nat, Eric, Chris, Wendy, Damian and my divorce lawyers at Carr and Co. To Pippa-la Doube for kindly giving her permission to include her article *"To all the Men in My Life From My Feminine Heart: a Letter of Gratitude"*.

A very warm and heartfelt thanks to the best friends a woman could ask for - Anita, Fenella and Bec. To my family - my daughter Cait, my parents, my brothers and their families. Thank you all from the bottom of my heart.

I would also like to acknowledge and thank my ex-husband for the personal learning's that I received out of the marriage. But most of all from this union came the most precious gift my daughter Cait. For that I will always be grateful.

ABOUT THE AUTHOR

Gaina Radford is a highly-established and gifted speaker and counsellor. Specialising in relationship breakdowns, sexual awareness and personal development, Gaina has enlightened many people from all corners of the world with her insightful coaching and teaching practices. Now, she has released her first book, The Exit Strategy: Plan. Recover. Thrive. Finally, here is a book to help you navigate your way through a relationship breakdown, providing helpful information to support you every step of the way during the tumultuous journey. When you don't know what to do next, you need a strategy - The Exit Strategy.

Gaina shares her years of intense research and personal experiences about divorce, recovering and thriving. The Exit Strategy will be many things to many people - it is empowering, educational, motivational and inspiring.